DREAM GREATNESS
BE UNSTOPPABLE

Gene Bittel,
You have the
gift of communication.
Be GREAT!
Wilson Hunter
4/14/07

DREAM GREATNESS BE UNSTOPPABLE

*Principles for Success
and Being True to Your Dreams*

WILLIAM HUNTER

An Inspiration/Leadership/Self-help Book

Published by William Hunter

HP Books may be purchased for educational, business or sales professional use. For more information, please write:

Hunter Publication
P. O. Box 5362
Capitol Heights, MD 20792
www.hunterinspires.com

The Library of Congress has catalogued the soft cover edition as follows:
Hunter, William J.
Dream Greatness Be Unstoppable:
Principles for Success and Being True to Your Dreams/
William J. Hunter

African-Americans-life skills guides and Psychology; Applied Psychology; Business Communication – General; Business Life – Inspirational; Careers; Excellence; General Motivation; Guides; Health and Wellness; Health, Mind and Body; Interpersonal Relations; Inspiration; Personal Growth – General; Personal Transformation; Success; Personal Transformation; Psychology and Social Sciences; Self-Help; Social Psychology and Interactions; Success; advice on careers and achieving success.

ISBN-13: 978-0-9792263-0-4
ISBN-10: 0-9792263-0-9

Copyright @ 2007 by William J. Hunter
All Rights Reserved.
Printed in the United States of America
March 2007
First Edition

PRAISE FOR WILLIAM HUNTER

"Change is often difficult. And, you are entitled to remain the same for an entire lifetime. But, if you are willing to step out beyond the excuses, if you are tired of living under your expectations, if you can consider taking just one small step everyday toward the greatness within yourself, *Dream Greatness Be Unstoppable* will take you to your destination."

-Gerri Pinkston, PhD
Psychologist and Educator

"On Point...*Dream Greatness Be Unstoppable* is a truly motivating and insightful tool that provides readers with an influential step by step road map to greatness. William Hunter has succeeded in delivering an instrument of high quality that is concise, to the point and equally unforgettable."

-Valerie M. Thomas, MBA, PMP

"*Dream Greatness Be Unstoppable* is quite simply the best common sense approach to successful living I've read. The positivity and the self-awareness needed for greatness he conveys in every chapter challenges us to take a look at ourselves and improve. This book can be a tool for all. It can be enjoyed as easy reading or as a reference with the user friendly table of contents. This book is destined for NY Times Bestseller's List."

-Garbo Watson Hearne,
Book Seller, Pyramid Art, Books and Custom Framing

"An important and approachable book that is likely to resonate with most audiences. William Hunter delves into the meaning and purpose of life from a grounded perspective. He talks to people where they are today... and makes a compelling case for personal change. His message is infused with inspiration and conviction."

-Mara Lopez,
Government Training Officer

"A great read...since high school William Hunter has been holding our attention with his motivational humor and anecdotes about being a standout player on and off the basketball court, now he is sharing his wit and wisdom with the world....*Dream Greatness Be Unstoppable* is thought-provoking."

-Edward "Sonny" White Jr.,
Owner, Tre Shirts, Custom Screenprinting, Embroidery and Designs

"The topic of greatness and excellence is one which William Hunter obviously feels a great deal of passion about. In this time when we all tend to be workaholics and over-schedulers, and civility is on the decline, it's good to be reminded to take a deep breath and reassess what is truly important in our lives."

-Saundra Kee Borges,
Attorney and former City Manager

"William Hunter encourages our spirits to stay the course, believing in and shining our own God-given light for ourselves and all the world to appreciate. This book is about faith affirmed and lived. We all need to receive this kind of encouragement many times in our lives. There's hope and healing here for each of us."

-Margaret Musgrove, PhD
Administrator, Loyola College and author of *The Spider Weaver: A Legend of Kente Cloth*, and *Ashanti to Zulu African Traditions*

"It takes courage to change passion and character for the pursuit of our convictions. William Hunter's book is thoughtful and inspiring…it is a must read for anyone committed to "Dreaming Greatness" and being unstoppable."

-Maryland State Senator Verna L. Jones,
Chair, Legislative Black Caucus of Maryland

ACKNOWLEDGEMENTS

The writing of this book has been a challenging and evolutionary experience for me personally. It was an undertaking that I could not have completed without the help and support of a number of "important people" in my life.

From a personal perspective, thanks first to Sarah C. Hunter, my mother. Mom, you have been a guiding force in my life. It is your belief in and support of me that gave me the courage to dream dreams, and to pursue my dreams, one of which was this book. Thanks also to my family, Mamie Ruth James, Alex Carr, Usha Carr, Ezekiel Carr, and Ben Hunter for believing and encouraging their brother. Although my father, Arthur Hunter, my sister Mattie Pearl Carr Garrison and my brother, Carlton D. Hunter have each passed on, their lasting memories gave me the enthusiasm and audacity to complete this book. I miss you and will continue to carry your love with me everyday.

Thanks to my friends, my network and those of you who have written and called with comments, suggestions, and criticism, thankfully not too much of the latter. I do read each and every message and even attempt to reply to them all eventually and all are appreciated.

I have had the pleasure of working with many outstanding colleagues who served as guideposts along the way as I completed each chapter. Each, in his or her own way, motivated me to continue to seek excellence. Representing several regions across the land, from Maryland to the District of Columbia, from Connecticut to Florida, Virginia, California, Georgia, Texas, New York, New Jersey, Pennsylvania, North Carolina, South Carolina and Germany — you know who you are — you are the best team in the world.

Finally, I must return thanks to Mother Earth which sustains me. I return thanks to the rivers and streams which supply us with water. I return thanks to the corn fields and her sisters, the beans and squashes, which sustain and nourish. I return thanks to the moon and the stars for their light when the sun no longer shines. I return thanks to the sun that gives light and life to the earth with a beneficent eye. And, most importantly, I return thanks to God who embodies all goodness and who directs all things for the good of His children.

Last, but not least, thanks to Mary E.B. Smith, my editorial consultant and Teri Saunier, owner of Material Graphics, for my cover design, photograph image, color and interior design to help communicate what my book is about. For being involved with this book, your input was invaluable and made *Dream Greatness Be Unstoppable* more compelling and a much better book. Thank you, each of you, who stood beside me and with me, as I went about writing this book.

CONTENTS

Introduction 1

Chapter 1
Life's Purpose 5
Purpose, Passion, Dreams and Success 5
Unlocking Your Dreams and Releasing Your Greatness 11
Principles 13

Chapter 2
The Pursuit of Excellence 15
Be Excellent and Be Unstoppable 15
Find Your Passion and Be Unstoppable 18
Imagination Creates Purpose/Possibilities 23
Be Personally Competent and Socially Intelligent 24
Principles 27

Chapter 3
Thinking the Right Thoughts to Succeed 29
Envision Your Future, Your Life Will Reflect What You Think 29
The Power of Thought 32
Thinking for a Change…Commit to Happiness 34
Emotional and Rational Thinking 36
Multi-tasking Affects Ability to Think 38
Mind Over Matter – Think and Succeed 40
Empowering Thought and Happiness 42
Principles 45

Chapter 4
Likability, Magnetism and Success 47
Likability as the First Impression 47
Likability Supports Relationship-Building 48
Building Self-Awareness to Influence Others 51

Personality Drives Relationship Success 54
A Mind Thing, Female and Male Approach to Thinking 56
Personality Helps in Making Decisions 61
Tap into Your Dormant Power, Fear 67
Reaching Your Potential and the 80/20 Rule 68
Principles 69

Chapter 5
Self-trust, Awareness and Fearlessness 71
Trust in Yourself 71
Trust is Necessary to Unlocking Dreams 76
Belief in a Just World 78
Never Accept Defeat...Acknowledge and Forgive Yourself and Others .81
Principles 82

Chapter 6
Positive Multi-dimensional Healing 83
Healing Attitudes 83
Smile With Your Eyes 88
Nonverbal Emotional Communications 90
Live Cheerfully 92
Be Calm 96
Persistence and Willpower 100
Friendship and Love 105
Imagination and Creativity 106
Juggling Adversely Affects Learning and Memory 107
Self-assessment and Positive Self-talk 114
Principles 115

Chapter 7
Letting Go of Clutter in Your Mind 117
Positive Thinking Makes Good Memories 117
Letting the Past Go 118
Embracing Hard Times and Enhancing Achievement 119
Clean Up Clutter 120
Principles 122

Chapter 8
Road Map to Success 123
Plan to Succeed or Fail to Plan 123
Discover the Secrets for Creating Success 127
Dreaming Big to Overcome Circumstances 129
Words that Speak Success 132
Surviving in a Hostile Environment 135
Laughter and Humor Therapy 136
Networking 101 Win Relationships 140
Principles 142

Chapter 9
Health, Wellness and Success 143
Interactions Between Your Mind and Body 143
For Mind Sake, Listen to Your Body 146
Nutritional Knowledge, Health and Wellness 148
Everyday Behavior and Lifestyle Practice 151
Principles 154

Chapter 10
Cultivating Gratitude 155
Gratitude and Self-Reflection 155
Be Focused, Joyful and Grateful 156
Count Your Blessings Everyday and Be Thankful 160
Carpe Diem and Seize Your Success 162
Principles 163

Conclusion 165
Principles 169

Afterthought 171

INTRODUCTION

"Every morning in Africa, a gazelle wakes up. It knows it must outrun the fastest lion or it will be killed. Every morning in Africa, a lion wakes up. It knows it must run faster than the slowest gazelle or it will starve. It doesn't matter whether you're a lion or a gazelle – when the sun comes up, you'd better be running."

— Anonymous

The sun comes up every day. You must be relentless in daring to dream greatness if you want to be unstoppable and have greatness. There are no restrictions on achieving your dreams and greatness except self imposed ones limiting your ability to dream great things for your life. The more you can dream, the more you can accomplish. Dreams come before reality, dreaming greatness leads to being unstoppable living life with unlimited potential and great achievement. The greatest achievements always take place in the framework of great expectations. If you don't have a dream, how are you going to make it come true?

Everybody has a dream of greatness about themselves. Everybody has an image, a picture in their mind of what their life would look like if their dreams came true. It is not egotistical or self-centered to dream and tap your imagination. You must dream beyond what you think is possible to achieve success beyond your reach. The secret to successful people is that they never lose focus, never stop reaching, never stop striving to overcome and accomplish their goals. Greatness requires self mastery which starts with assessing what's important to you. Some of the most brilliant people in the world struggle to do one simple thing correctly, knowing and understanding themselves. Do you live to work or work to live? Do you have a road map for achieving career success? It all starts with learning why you work in the first place. The most successful people dream of opportunities and direct their own greatness, no matter what they do for a living. You can be successful, right now. It begins by dreaming greatness. In my dreams of greatness, I'm an author. My book is the first of many profound best selling books. Dream your dreams today.

If you could read one good book in the next three hundred and sixty-five days, you have it. *Dream Greatness Be Unstoppable* is a motivational guide to mastering your inner self and the "people dimension" of your careers to help you tighten your grasp of people skills, deepen your understanding of common needs and differences, improve your ability to be inspired and inspire peak performance from others to ensure your success and optimal organizational effectiveness. The premise of this book is to challenge and inspire you to discover fresh principles and perspectives, and to make appropriate applications that will help you achieve a higher level of personal and professional effectiveness. Dream Greatness Be Unstoppable focuses on enhancing personal effectiveness, creating inspiration, enjoyment and success by providing insights into tapping the leader within you to sense, understand, and apply the power of your emotions as a source of energy, creativity and influence.

Some individuals may find excellence as a topic less appealing than entertainment or physical sports or something with a social emphasis. I hope you are pleasantly surprised as you peruse the chapters of this book. Being excellent isn't required in order to achieve the position of your dreams, but it helps. Excellence greatly increases your chances of success in your chosen field and in life. While excellence may seem to be superficial and easy to implement, it is not. It is difficult to make real and permanent changes in your personality. The process of becoming excellent takes years. Do not let that intimidate you, however. Remember, as Confucius says, "the journey of a thousand miles begins with a single step." Excellence, like dancing, writing or golf, is something which must be practiced.

As leaders within our society (and every one of us is a leader), we must strive for excellence. In order to truly make a contribution in this fast-paced, ever changing world, we must continue to be competitive. We must try to make a difference. Excellence is a concept, a thought, an idea, — that should be exhibited in our actions. Nelson Mandela stated, "Education is the most powerful weapon which you can use to change the world." James Baldwin wrote, "For nothing is fixed, forever and forever and forever, it is not fixed; the earth is always shifting, the light is always changing, the sea does not cease to grind down rock. Generations do not cease to be born, and we are responsible to them because we are the only witnesses they have." George Bernard Shaw wrote, "Some see things as they are and say, "Why?" I dream of things that never were and say, "Why not?" John F. Kennedy said, "Change is the law of life. And those who look only to the past or present are certain to miss the future." Leo Tolstoy wrote, "Everyone thinks of changing the world, but no one thinks of changing himself."

Life is progress not a stopping point and change is inevitable. We may have growth in one part of our life and not in another. Excellence reminds us that there is always a need for growth. In order to grow, we must change the way in which we think. We must change our actions. Ultimately, we change our outcomes and move closer to excellence.

Introduction

We each must strive for excellence as a part of our life long journey, displaying new attitudes and the new behaviors associated with them, sowing seeds of excellence, potential seed for change along the way. As a former standout basketball player, I had to learn to play defense rather offense, learn how to stay focused when other people invaded my space, learn multiple plays, call frequent huddles, keep score during the game, turn hecklers into fans and always practice as if it were a real game. As a result, I won a State Basketball championship. By doing your personal best today, one day you will harvest success at a great level of excellence. Your striving for excellence will be reflected in your goals, values, beliefs, and faith. As you strive for excellence, you'll influence others along the way. Even if you feel trapped in a dissatisfying job or a seemingly insignificant career, your attitude can make all the difference in how you view your situation. When you do find your passion, your true calling, your work will be a source of satisfaction and fulfillment—and you will be proud to sign your name to it.

Excellence begins with one's intent, passion and purpose. Excellence begins within us and it is in each of us. With excellence, we design our own success. You deserve success. Dream a dream and make a promise to yourself that you can and will keep. Get your "game on." Become excellent in all that you do. Begin to manifest change in your life.

I am personally convinced that each of us can make a difference in this world. We can each become a catalyst for change in the lives of those around us. Inspire, motivate and influence others and leave excellence as your personal legacy.

DREAM GREATNESS BE UNSTOPPABLE

1
LIFE'S PURPOSE

"What happens to a dream deferred? Does it dry up like a raisin in the sun?"

— Langston Hughes, *Harlem Renaissance-Langston Hughes*

Purpose, Passion, Dreams and Success

Some people know their purpose but aren't moving forward on it because something is holding them back. Our biggest issues are all based in fear of failure, of the unknown and of rejection. We may even have a fear of success and the responsibility that comes with it. I believe that we all want a good life, not just in the material sense, but one with purpose. Purpose is that internal drive that gives meaning to the things we do each day. My purpose is writing, speaking, and talking to people with a message of hope.

Success calls for a high level of commitment, not to a particular course, but to learning and growing in general to make valid and worthwhile contributions to society and in reality, ourselves. Many people are committed to being successful but commitment does not equal purpose. We need to know our purpose in life, what are we here for? Whatever our purpose may be in life, we cannot fulfill that purpose by ourselves. We cannot get to the rooftop without a ladder and we need other people to enables us to fulfill our purpose. We are not an island, we cannot live by ourselves in spite of how big our egos may get. We need associations, friendships, companionships, and partnerships in our lives. Also we need to be healthy. We need good health to achieve our purpose.

Every day, we need more people to do random acts of love or kindness for someone. Doing this keeps us connected to the human experience. These acts would multiply over and over to thousands of caring acts of love. Together with a road map, including critical information with people working on small group projects connecting their purpose to others involved in the community, almost any problem would be solvable.

My purpose in writing, speaking, and talking to people with a message of hope is about discovery rooted in the sense that life is an adventure and worthwhile things come from being free, and breaking loose from traditional rules. In each choice we make, we have the potential for discovering something new each day. In making choices, we must take responsibility for our choices and not hide behind rules or procedures. We need to think for ourselves. This is a difficult standard to live by because we want to identify with others rather than break away from them. Discovery brings pain as well as joy. Purpose is about being excellent, the belief that excellent performance is the supreme good in our lives. Purpose is about being excellent which means we will turn down offers and opportunities rather than compromise our standards. Purpose is altruism and inspirational in supporting social change motivated by compassion and self-sacrifice not only for charities and some social groups but also a range of businesses that exist to serve their customers. When we operate on a higher level, we are in touch with our purpose and act on that purpose, influencing people rather than trying to operate in a value-free sphere.

I believe that people who pursue their life's purpose and passion can make a living on their passion. Many of us set ourselves up for failure because we don't figure out our life's purpose and passion. By discovering your purpose and passion, then structuring your passion into a business strategy, you can become a "passionpreneur" with products or services and profits. The first step is to figure out your purpose in life. Your purpose could be creative, helping/teaching, leading or guiding. Creative people are artistic; saviors like to heal or fix; gurus are teachers, coaches or information providers; and guides are leaders, such as Rev. Dr. Martin Luther King Jr., Malcolm X, Sojourner Truth and Harriet Tubman. Determining your purpose helps you to pick the career path best suited for your dreams or ultimate aims. For example, someone who loves to cook might think that starting a restaurant is the best option. But if you see your life's purpose as being a guru rather than a creator, then starting a cooking school would be a better choice. Our passion will help us fulfill our purpose. We have to ask ourselves, what do we love to do and we would do it without money being involved? We are often reluctant to talk about our passion because we fear that others will laugh at us. Once we have identified our passion, the next step is to dream up a list of products or services based on that passion and purpose. Examples are a book, food, art, invention or services, such as lecturing, performing or coaching.

The reason that many people fail is that they quit too soon or they pursue a career path that doesn't fit their life's purpose. There are going to be ups and downs and failures but everything that happens to us is working toward our benefit. I believe that we live in a creative, supportive universe. As change agents, we are being called to a new level of awareness. I believe in the prospect of a shift in the quality of lives as we each claim our authentic selves and really begin to live life. Experience has shown that dreaming dreams works. It is quite possible to prove that circumstances and events follow thoughts. Here are the reasons why dreaming dreams produces results.

Our thoughts have power, and the universal laws cause its tremendous power to manifest itself on our behalf. Our mind is our partner in creating our life. Each thought, action and event in the universe is connected, and each influences the other. Each thought and action causes reactions and repercussions. Everything in the Universe is energy and your thoughts, as part of this body of energy, work with the creative Universal energy and interact with it. Thoughts are like a magnet, they attract similar thoughts and circumstances. Thinking one thought invites into your mind more similar thoughts and ideas. These thoughts tend to attract circumstances that are in accordance with them.

As you think, your dreams radiate from your mind and are transmitted to other minds. Thoughts that sink into your subconscious mind drive you into corresponding action. Each thought you think arouses an associated emotion. Strong thoughts energized by emotions generate more energetic and definite action than weak thoughts. If you constantly feed your mind with negative thoughts and words, your mind will produce negative conditions, but if you feed your mind with positive thoughts and words it will produce positive conditions and circumstances.

Achieving your goals requires answering the right questions. Once you answer the first question... once you know why you are here...then you must answer larger questions. But what is your purpose and how do you identify it? Your purpose is embedded in your response to these questions.

- What is your purpose in life? Do you have a strong sense of purpose, passion and direction driven by your personal mission statement?
- What is your vision in life?
- What is the vision that is bigger than you or even larger than your own needs?
- What must you do to achieve your purpose driven life...your best life now?
- Do you have a personal mission statement?
- Do you feel anchored to live your life's purpose?

- Do you understand the importance of purpose and mission in your life?
- Do you have the insight you need to live what's most important to you... every single day...for the rest of your life?
- What do you believe you "naturally" do best in life?
- What are you good at?
- What is unique about you? What unique gifts, talents and skills do you bring to this world?
- What are your greatest talents?
- If you could have any kind of job, what would it be?
- Do you do time management and do you spend too much time on things that simply don't matter?
- Do you have the ability and skills to convert your dreams and wishes into crystal-clear future expectations so you never again waste a single "tomorrow?"
- Do you have the ability to make difficult decisions with a clear conscious so you are always focused on what is important to you?
- What level do you want to reach professionally or in your career?
- Is there any knowledge you want to acquire in particular? What information and skills will you need to achieve other goals?
- How much do you want to earn by what stage?
- What are you doing to sabotage yourself or hold yourself back?
- What do you love to do?
- What gives you the greatest joy?
- What do you want to accomplish before you die?
- Do you live from your heart and follow your dreams so you truly live what you value most?
- What are your current motivation, values, and virtues?
- Have you identified the personal values that will guide your ultimate success?

- Do you balance your personal time, your career goals and other important things in your life?
- Do you look back on each and every day with pride and satisfaction... rather than with regrets and recriminations?
- Are you experiencing more fun and abundance in your life today?
- What specific issues represent your life challenges?
- How much of your life is controlled by your personality? Inspired by your soul?
- What underlying semi-conscious motives run your life?
- How much do you value your life?
- Do you treasure each day? Or do you allow each new day to come and go, a carbon copy of the one before, basically unnoticed, unappreciated and under-used?
- Are you stuck on the road to nowhere?
- Are you too busy to enjoy life?
- Are you not getting the results you want?
- Do you have personal goals and do you set goals for yourself?
- Do you feel that you are under too much stress, anxiety and have chaos in your life?
- Do you consciously choose how you spend the precious time of your life or lose time to mundane tasks or to meeting other people's expectations?
- Do you maintain the intention and attention to critical goals and task you need for success?
- Do you track your goals and celebrate your achievements?
- Do you tap into your own intuition and inner wisdom?
- Are you slowing down to make fewer mistakes, and have more laughter and fun?
- Are you developing self trust and self confidence, courage and faith?
- Do you have physical energy?

- Do you have the ability to set goals?
- Do you have the ability to make plans?
- Do you have the ability to prioritize your actions?
- Do you have the ability to synergize with others?
- Do you have the ability to optimize your time?
- Are you willing to improve over the next six months to make the biggest difference in your life?
- What do you really want from life?
- Do you want to achieve any artistic goals? If so, what?
- Is any part of your mindset holding you back? Is there any part of the way that you behave that upsets you? If so, what goal will you set to improve your behavior or find a solution to the problem?
- If not already, do you want to be a parent? If so, how are you going to be a good parent?
- How do you want to be seen by a partner or members of your extended family?
- Are there any athletic goals you want to achieve, or do you want good health deep into old age? What steps are you going to take to achieve this?
- How do you want to enjoy yourself? How will you ensure that some of your life is for you?
- Do you want to make the world a better place by your existence? If so, how?

For many of us, success, however we choose to measure it, comes at a price. We often find we can not spend time with our families due to job constraints. Or we can not eat properly due to the time pressures placed on us. It is possible to achieve success at whatever level we choose, and it is possible to do this while maintaining a healthy perspective. There will always be trade-offs and compromises, but these can be done in the context of a larger picture, a picture that has been planned to give due attention to all of its facets of our life with a balanced lifestyle. Creating a balanced lifestyle is about achieving a sense of balance in all areas of your life. Whatever you choose, create positive changes in key areas of your life. I believe that we can work on the picture and maintain balance while we do it. The keys to balance and success begin with a thought. The starting place on the path to making your dreams a reality is creating a balanced lifestyle. A balanced life style allow you to gather the motivation and energy you need to take small but daily steps toward the definition and fulfillment of your dreams. Once defined, the next step in the process of dream fulfillment may involve a good look at your belief system. Then ask yourself if you deserve to take the time needed to reach your goals? Are you willing to take the necessary risks, and spend the time, energy and money to realize your dream?

When people do not succeed in making their dream a reality, it is because they give up. Fear of success can hold you back. Dreams are goals with deadlines. Goals are the keys to motivation and extraordinary living with unlimited potential. "Look at your dream. Set goals that are realistic; stay on task by doing just one small thing everyday to bring you closer to the fulfillment of your dream. Crowd out negative thoughts by replacing them with positive thoughts such as "I will make my dream come true." You have within you all that you need to manifest your dream. Slowly, step-by-step, your dream will become reality before your eyes. Too many of us are living lives of quiet extreme anxiety. Only you can name your dream and make it come true. Don't be thrown off course by disparaging comments made by those who denigrate your dream. Frequently these remarks come from people who are afraid to pursue their own dreams. Create a space and time for your dreams each day. Trust your intuition on your journey. Your search for your purpose is open to the full spectrum of possibilities. Your purpose can be anything there are no boundaries or limitations to the manner in which your purposes is realized.

Unlocking Your Dreams and Releasing Your Greatness

While growing up in New Haven, Connecticut, I aspired to become a professional basketball player. Although I never realized that dream, I developed as a standout motivational player, writer, speaker, and subject matter expert presenter to people with a message of hope, a driving ambition and attitude that refuses to quit. As a motivational optimist, I focus on ways to help people meet the challenges of our changing demographics by understanding the power of passion and purpose.

I discovered that words send messages and unless we speak positively about ourselves, we may be giving ourselves negative messages. Many people do. These negative thoughts or messages make us feel bad about ourselves, lower our self-esteem and contribute to health problems. Many of our messages have been with us for some time, we may have learned them when we were young. I wasn't satisfied with what I learned and I decide to look at the other side of the coin by looking at my thoughts or words in a new light. This led me to understanding that there is a natural energetic quality to any affirming or supportive thoughts, words or behavior. Simply stated, our thoughts, words or behavior are supportive of our overall health. According to my research, the way we speak dramatically influences our mental health and ultimately our success.

"Excellence Talking" is a system of using common words positively in our ever day life. For example, we should use words such as: appreciative, approving, brilliant, confident, flexible, giving, harmonious, helpful, honest, joyful, kind, nurturing, optimistic, praising, respectful, significant, spiritual, tolerant, unselfish and valuing which are affirming and supportive words that will help us maintain our mental and physical health. When we use negative words with destructive connotation our health is similarly affected. Most healthcare professionals acknowledge the power of "excellence" positive thinking. Few people know how to put excellence thoughts into action. Scientific studies have shown that speech influences your success in any field...and in life. Studies now prove that people who are "excellence positive talkers" live longer, healthier lives, and achieve their goals faster. "Problems" become "challenges." "I will try" becomes "I will." "I will have to" is replaced with "I will be glad to." "I am not worth anything" becomes "I am a valuable person." "I have never accomplished anything" becomes "I have accomplished many things." "I do not deserve a good life" is replaced with "I deserve to be happy and healthy." "I am stupid" is replaced with "I am smart." Employees who communicate positively and enjoy happy, fulfilling relationships work better. Excellence results from clear, positive communications.

If I refuse to allow fear or my history to imprison me. I have chosen a path of self-determination. When you stop holding your dreams and greatness captive, you strengthen your psychological immune system. You recognize your capacity to thrive in spite of the hardships that have come your way, and watch your life begin to mirror your more empowered self concept and your vision for your life. As a result, you no longer need to blame anyone or your self for your failures or unhappiness. As we forgive ourselves, let go of blame, we lighten up, move on and feel an inner peace. I decided to change my thoughts and eliminate habitual, self-limiting thinking. Instead of focusing on how my life has been, I place my attention on how I want my life to be. As you let go of your past, you free yourself to live the life you truly desire. Stop holding your dreams and greatness captive, and discover the unlimited potential for joy that awaits you.

Principles

- Happiness is not self-indulgence but a commitment to your purpose.
- When we are purposeful, we are happier and at peace.

DREAM GREATNESS BE UNSTOPPABLE

2
THE PURSUIT OF EXCELLENCE

"Mr. Meant-to has a friend, his name is Didn't-Do. Have you met them? They live together in a house called Never-Win. And I am told that it is haunted by the Ghost of Might-have-Been."

— Marva Collins, *Marva Collins' Way*

Be Excellent and Be Unstoppable

In my role as an Excellence Coach, I have worked with extremely successful people who want to get even better. Intellectually, they realize that the leadership behavior that was associated with yesterday's results may not be the behavior that is needed to achieve tomorrow's success. Research shows the benefit of optimism and positive frames of mind are huge. The "contradiction of success" occurs because we need to change before we have to change. Maybe we don't know that we have to change, that we must change or we are hoping that we won't have to change. But the reality is that we must embrace change or deal with the consequences. There are a variety of reasons why successful people succeed. Successful people have a high need for self-determination. Successful people have a unique distaste for feeling restricted. Successful people not only believe that they can achieve, they believe that they will achieve. Successful leaders communicate with an overall sense of self-confidence. Successful people tend to have a positive interpretation of their past performance. You can be successful by focusing on positive, measurable, long-term change in your behavior.

The emerging diverse optimists who are needed in today's workplace embody qualities that include self-awareness, flexibility, self-confidence, initiative, resiliency, and adaptability. Positive people shun pessimism, but they are attracted to optimism. Pessimism will sap energy out of your life. Pessimism will drive creative people away, and you will be left alone. Pessimism is the toxic soil where worry, fear and anxiety sprout and choke your life's dreams. Tomorrow looks hopeful.

Optimism is an emotional competence that leads to increased productivity. We demonstrate our excellence by our performance. Excellence is essential in rising above the crowd and in providing others what they want. We benefit from excellence by improving our self esteem and self-worth, as well as how others view us. Excellence is a reflection and relates how we feel about ourselves, our attitude, confidence, self-esteem, self-worth, and pride in our abilities. Excellence is essential for business or personal success.

Excellence is never a question of can we be excellent. Excellence requires two critical skills:

- Excellence builds our confidence, the feeling that we are sure that we can complete a challenging task. Excellence means we are sure of our skills and ability to succeed in any endeavor in life.

- Excellence is an internal determination of how sure we are of our skills. Excellence is being able to succeed based on a track record of succeeding in other areas of life. The feeling of excellence provides self-confidence which is learned and can be passed from one area of life to another.

The price of excellence is commitment. Excellence will be guaranteed when we begin to incorporate mental strategies that all peak performers utilize. Excellence as a strategy means making choices, not excuses.

- Living up to your potential by committing to excellence.
- Dreaming big dreams.
- Committing to life-long learning and growth.
- Developing buoyancy and bounce back.
- Developing a positive mental attitude.
- Identifying your area of excellence.

Now is the time to be about excellence. When you are about excellence, you understand your personal strengths and weaknesses and you are willing to work hard to make yourselves better at what you do. Excellence is about constantly working on ourselves. If we must work eight hours a day for survival then every hour over that should go toward excellence.

Excellence requires a sense of urgency, a bias for action. Where ever we are in life, we need to begin excellence today. Excellence and success means we do first things first and second things not at all. Excellence is the most valuable use of our time right now.

Excellence is a choice. The circumstances that surround our life are not important, how we respond to those circumstances is the critical difference between excellence and mediocrity, success and failure.

Excellence begins with self-confidence. Excellence develops and maintains credibility and enables us to avoid making careless comments about subjects on which we are not fully informed and avoid being associated with projects with a low likelihood of success. Excellence helps us to act confidently when in high stress situations and assists us in coping with problems. Excellence allows us to recognize team members' or colleagues' concerns and to be an effective listener to their concerns and uncertainties. Excellence avoids threatening the self-esteem of team members or colleagues.

I wasn't born with excellence or personal talent. I developed excellence and talent through learning and experience. Like other people with incremental beliefs, I saw my abilities and personality traits as impressionable. When it comes to personal talent, I don't believe people are born with high levels of personal talent. Instead, I believe that personal talent can be developed. I define personal talent as developed expertise in the areas of self-awareness, personal decision making, and self-regulation. For most of us, developing personal talent has been largely informal and those who have developed expertise and talent have been largely self-taught. I believe that excellence and personal talent is so important to life satisfaction and success that we should be systematically teaching excellence, personal talent knowledge and skills in educational settings so more young people, especially those with high ability, develop excellence and personal talent.

Discover your excellence. Think about how you can excel and develop a language to describe and discuss your excellence and talents. The following describes my excellence and talents. The nouns include: achiever; activator; arranger; coach; communicator; deliberator; developer; discoverer; dreamer; experimenter; facilitator; futurist; goal setter; learner; motivator; opinionator; optimist; personality assessor; relator; self-regulator; self-talker; stress manager; talent evaluator; and time manager. The adjectives include: adaptability; analytical; trust; connectedness; discipline; empathy; fairness; focus; futuristic; ideation; inclusiveness; individuation; input; intellection; maximizer; positivity; responsibility; restorative; self-assurance; self-aware; self-efficacy; significance; and strategic. Excellence is found in the pursuit of excellence. The road to excellence is more challenging than anything else because it means not only being a genius at one aspect of life, but being excellent in life itself.

Excellence is awe-inspiring. The excellence in any organization begins with individuals within the organization. If the people are not excellent, the organization will not be excellent. As leaders, when we pursue excellence and it raises the standard for others to follower and reach for.

Now that you know excellence, what do you do? Begin by thanking people for the little things they do to help you to be excellent. Be gracious on your journey to excellence. Remember, you only find oil if you drill wells.

Dream Greatness Be Unstoppable is about the virtues of excellence. The term Excellence is often thrown around. Webster's Dictionary defines excellence as "the state of being exceptionally good in quality and character." The root word of excellence is "excel" which means "to be greater or to surpass others." Excellence in itself is exactly that, amazing. Whether in grace, beauty, or power, someone who has achieved the right of excellence is someone who shines brighter than others. Excellence is where you have perfected yourselves at whatever you are capable of, and still progressing beyond that point. Excellence is something of beauty, a finely tuned performance. Excellence is the feeling and emotion behind the surface. Excellence is the passion that you have about what you do.

Dream Greatness Be Unstoppable acknowledges, to be successful you have got to have a dream, a vision, a burning passion, an obsession. This dream, goal, obsession has to become your prime motivator. To get the things you want in life you need motivation, drive, energy and be in control of your emotions. Successful people have dreams, dreams will inspire and motivate you. Dreams will make you think. They will make you dream. Look at where you are today. Dream of where you want to be tomorrow. Then create an action plan to take you there.

You are just a few simple steps away from realizing your most sacred dreams and ultimate goals. *Dream Greatness Be Unstoppable* gives you all the energy and wisdom you'll ever need to de-stress and live with clarity and passion. Picture yourself enjoying the kind of life you know you deserve. Realize in days what it took you years to accomplish before. Well, this book provides an overview of a concept which controls our ability to direct the flow, energy, and intention of our emotions at will, regardless of the circumstances.

Find Your Passion and Be Unstoppable

Have you ever watched others achieve great success while you sit on the side-line waiting going unnoticed and whimpering? Have you asked yourself, "Why not me?" Well it is time you know the answer, success and passion go hand in hand. We live in a very competitive time that if you're not doing something that you're passionate about, you just won't have the energy required to drive you ahead to become successful and unstoppable at what you do. You can be skilled but skill without talent is never going to win out over ability infused with passion. No matter what anyone else may say, think or do; find your passion, let your passion guide you in life and be unstoppable. It was my passion that was the driving force in writing my book *Dream Greatness Be Unstoppable*. I dreamed about writing and being a guru or guide I actually did it! I wanted to share strategies and views on how to become successful and what is important to being successful. The result is this body of work; reflecting on personal accounts from interesting and successful individuals. Passion alone won't get you to the top of your game. Deliberate goal setting along with other essential tools will help to fuel your passion to success. Your goals will drive your behavior, pull your behavior and push your behavior in a particular direction. And if you have passion behind the goal, you have energy to make it happen and with focus and persistence be unstoppable.

Everyone has dreams, regardless of our age, social or economic status. Dreams are something we want to have. Dreams are important. Dreams provide us a vision for our future and help us make decisions about how we want to live our lives. Dreams give us hope, and they inspire us. Being a dreamer is great when you take hold of the dream and move it into your purpose and passion. For many people clarifying their life's purpose becomes the key to unlocking their passion. The passion becomes the fuel that propels them forward in expressing their life purpose, often in extraordinary ways beyond anything they would have considered before.

People living with passion and on purpose become unstoppable, particularly the longer they live true to their passion and purpose and the more they allow both to shape their lives. People without clarity of passion and purpose often find themselves stuck in life, like a high powered automobile without any fuel. Living a life in which you are regularly expressing your purpose and allowing it to shape your decisions, your thoughts, feelings and actions is simply a whole lot more fulfilling. A life on purpose is filled with meaning, and people on purpose realize they are making a difference in the world simply by being in the world.

If you can do this, then you will have lived your dream even if you didn't. Your dream is also closely related to your core values, and getting in touch with those values help keep your dreams alive. Core values are an integral part of your life purpose. When you are living a life on purpose, you are living a value-based life, rather than a lifestyle-based life. People who know their passion and life purpose, and are living it, have a renewed zest for life. For most people, it's very difficult to answer. Many people are not following their passion because they are creatively blocked or paralyzed by fear. Uncover your true passion and find real happiness.

Passion is a rich, soulful emotion. Passion is an internal experience not an external event. Our busy, hectic lives disconnects us from our feelings. And, when we act from this "unfeeling" place, it's impossible to connect with our passions.

Emotional intelligence includes personality variables such as passion, happiness, extraversion and openness to experience. Happiness has been positively linked to success, including job productivity. It is associated with positive health and programs designed to improve performance, relationship quality, and general well-being. Our happiness depends on our ability to please at least ourselves. People are reluctant to use their own passion, happiness as the standard by which to judge the events in their lives because we let others define or affect what brings us happiness. Happy people deliberately do things that lead them to happiness. Being happy requires you define your life in your own terms and then throw your whole heart into living your life to the fullest. Your happiness will improve your self-esteem and high self-esteem leads to greater happiness. Happy moods promote health by boosting self-efficacy, optimism, and efforts to battle illness.

We need passion and other emotions to survive. Love allows us to bond and develop meaningful relationships. Emotional Intelligence is about becoming attuned to your emotions and the emotions of others, and using this information to increase happiness and harmony within yourself and your relationships. We may not be aware of our emotional triggers. Emotional Intelligence provides an awareness of what's going on in your body. New research shows that ninety-five percent of our decisions, emotions, behavior and actions are unconscious. Emotional Intelligence, like consulting, is about bringing the unconscious to the conscious. In consulting, we work with clients to uncover their core values and tame the voice of the inner critic, and these two things increase self-awareness substantially. Emotional Intelligence skills can easily be learned and improved. As leaders in our own right, we should set the standards for excellence. Successful organizations only want to hire excellent employees.

If we are overweight, we must find the passion for losing weight and work on it. As the saying goes, "no pain, no gain." Making mistakes is the key to making progress. Mistakes are not just golden opportunities for learning. You are not going to meet many perfect people in life. Perfect people are in the cemetery. The time to change is today not tomorrow. We have within us the power to create the life we desire.

Passion drives success in life. Passion, or love, is a normal concept in fields where compassion is second nature; for example, in healthcare and teaching.

Spirituality is a tool which helps you to meet your needs. It should be part of organizational culture. Organizations are realizing that they could become more successful by meeting their members' needs and allowing them to express their spirituality. Spirituality is a cultural phenomenon that influences organizational behavior. We all have spirituality, even if it be a nihilistic or materialistic spirituality. People expect organizations to cultivate some type of spirituality within their members in order to produce high quality products and services. Spirituality affects our emotional intelligence and is reflected or translated as workplace compassion, compassion for people and ethical leadership. Spirituality in business and work means making decisions and conducting oneself in a way that cares for people and the world we live in. In the past, male-oriented performance management, financial results, profits bottom-line organizations with dispassionate ideas and priorities have tended to dominate business. Conversely, love, compassion and spirituality are generally perceived to be female traits. Men are less likely than women to demonstrate loving, compassionate, spiritual behavior because of cultural and social expectations, especially when reinforced by the business traditions. Many bottom-line oriented successful business people owe much of their success to their unloving, dispassionate behavior. Where unloving dispassionate behavior exists in a business leader, whatever its cause, this unavoidably sets the tone for the whole organization to be unloving and uncaring, and devoid of spiritual awareness. Spirituality is a component of motivation and change. For businesses seeking to introduce social responsibility and compassion into their organizational culture, spirituality is a tool.

Increasing numbers of people are fed up with the selfish character of corporations and organizations and the way they conduct themselves. As a result, people expect change. Compassion and spirituality-consideration for people and the world we live in-whatever you choose to call it- is a relevant ethos in business and organizations. People need spiritual meaning as much as they need food and drink. Increasing numbers of people are advocating for greater compassion and spirituality. Female-oriented qualities and emotional intelligence strengths are important in improving the climate and the way we do business.

In business and in all of our relationships, we need passion as well as profit. We need ambition, sincerity, strength, innovation, optimism, and the never give up attitude. The premise to hold in mind is: success = (equals) effort x (times) ability x (times) attitude. Research indicates that emotional intelligence is a distinguishing factor in performance and leadership. Emotional competence is twice as important as purely cognitive abilities in all jobs in every field. It provides an advantage for success at the highest levels and leadership positions. There are many other laws that govern us at our different levels of being: Universal Laws of Nature, Spiritual Laws, Mental/Emotional Laws, Law of Love, Law of Forgiveness, Law of Abundance and Scientific Laws, Physical laws.

The focus of emotional intelligence is on using our minds; a series of skills, mostly having to do with social interaction and self-knowledge. High intelligence (IQ) is no guarantee of success, happiness, or virtue. Scholastic Aptitude Test (SAT) testing programs and academic grades are now being replaced with emotional intelligence and emotional competence to provide an objective method of screening individuals to find those best qualified for employment and promotion, training, or academic situation. In the future emotional intelligence may be used for screening preschoolers must meet minimum standards on emotional competence categories for admission to many private kindergartens. Our emotional intelligence determines our potential for learning the five elements upon which it is based: self-awareness, motivation, self-regulation, empathy and social skills or adeptness in relationships.

The distinction between book-smarts and people-smarts is most visible in the management and leadership problems organizations face today. Interpersonal ineptitude in leaders lowers everyone's performance. It wastes times, creates acrimony, corrodes motivation and commitment, builds hostility, mistrust, and apathy. Lacking self-control when under pressures, we fail poorly and are prone to moodiness and angry outbursts. Successful leaders remain calm under stress, confident and dependable in the heat of crisis. Successful leaders take responsibility by admitting their mistakes and take action to fix the problems. Successful leaders have high integrity, with a strong concern for the needs of their subordinates and colleagues, rather than giving a higher priority to impressing the boss. Moods and emotions play a central role in the leadership process. More specifically, emotional intelligence, the ability to understand and manage moods and emotions in self and others, contributes to effective leadership in organizations. There are four hierarchical abilities that lead to high emotional intelligence: (1) the accurate perception, appraisal, and expression of emotions; (2) generating feelings on demand when they can facilitate understanding of yourself or another person; (3) understanding emotions and the knowledge that can be derived from them; and (4) the regulation of emotion to promote emotional and intellectual growth. Emotional intelligent contributes to effective leadership by focusing on five essential elements of leader effectiveness: development of collective goals and objectives; instilling in others an appreciation of the importance of work activities; generating and maintaining enthusiasm, confidence, optimism, cooperation, and trust; encouraging flexibility in decision making and change; and establishing and maintaining a meaningful identity for an organization.

There is a negative relationship between management by-exception (passive) and the emotional intelligence. This includes components of emotional recognition and expression (in oneself), understanding of emotion, emotional management, emotional control, and other areas of emotional intelligence. There is a positive relationship between contingent rewards (a component of transactional leadership) and emotional intelligence. Emotional intelligence can be leveraged and applied in the areas of change management.

Emotional intelligence strongly relates to all components of transformational leadership, with the components of understanding of emotions (external) and emotional management the best predictors of this type of leadership style. Leadership emotional intelligence skills include self awareness, reflection, intuition, and compassion for yourself and others. These skills enhance emotional events in productive ways. Emotional intelligence provides for a deep understanding of one's emotions, strengths, weaknesses, needs, and drives. Emotional intelligence includes the propensity for reflection, the ability to adapt to changes, and allows you to say no to impulsive urges.

For example, we may believe we are smart, confident, humorous, energetic, having strong opinions, passionate, strong, detail oriented, quiet or quiet. Emotional intelligence is necessary for success in many ways: emotional self-awareness; accurate self-assessment; self-confidence; self-control; trustworthiness; conscientiousness; adaptability; achievement orientation; initiative; empathy; organizational awareness; developing others; service orientation; leadership; influence; communication; change catalyst; conflict management; building bonds; teamwork and collaboration.

Imagination Creates Purpose/Possibilities

Positive thinking is powerful and can be used to change and improve our lives. We can use the power of our imagination and mind to create what we want in our lives and then develop science to supports it. For example, in healthcare, the guided imagery method of using our imagination has being successful in helping people cope better with illness and stress. Untapped, failures of imagination has created bitter realities for too many people. Imagination, as any primary ability or talent, can be developed by training. We can improve our creative ability or our imagination by exercising it. The best creative exercises provide us with mental activity and material out of which we can form ideas. Experience can be firsthand or secondhand, such as reading, listening or watching. But firsthand experience is far superior. In developing our imagination, there is a special type of firsthand experience…self-reliance. During a dream, maybe your body responded with fear, joy, anger, or sadness all triggered by your imagination. Our imagination can be a very powerful resource in relieving stress, pain, and other unwanted symptoms.

We can learn to use the power of our imagination to produce calming, energizing, or healing responses in our body. We can decrease chronic muscle tension. We can decrease pain and the need for pain medications; improve comfort during medical, surgical, and dental procedures; reduce the length of labor and discomfort of childbirth; control bleeding. The mind can speed healing from injury, or skin conditions such as warts and psoriasis; ease sleep problems; improve management of chronic illnesses such as diabetes, asthma, lung, and heart disease; boost our immune function; increase sense of control and mastery; change bad habits and maintain healthy ones.

By using our imagination with guided imagery, we can deliberately focus our mind on a particular image. While imagery most often uses our sense of sight, we can also include the rich experiences of our mind's other senses. Adding smells, tastes, sounds, and other sensations makes the guided imagery experience more vivid and powerful. Some people with artistic traits are very visual, and easily see images with their mind's eye. But if your images aren't as vivid as a really great movie, don't worry. It's normal for imagery to vary in intensity. Remember, with guided imagery, we are always completely in control. We're the movie director. If we don't like a particular image, thought or feeling we can redirect our mind to something more comfortable. Imagination is a key to freedom. Imagination is a healer and supporter during trying times to discover and resolve behaviors, emotions and limiting beliefs on our journey to success.

Be Personally Competent and Socially Intelligent

It is not enough to be gifted, smart, or intelligent. The system and rules of the game have changed: we also have to be socially intelligent. Your brain is an instrument or social tool developed over time for promoting and guiding your social interactions and relationships. Your outgoing self or sociable brain allows you to transmit your desires and intentions which are your emotions to those around you and interpret their moods. We can work on our social intelligence, including social awareness (what we sense about others) and social facility (how we act on that awareness). We can develop skills such as "empathy," "attunement" in listening fully to others and "synchrony" using appropriate body language, such as nods and smiles, that allows conversation to flow.

Emotional intelligence (EI) or emotional competence (EQ) means different things to different people. Emotional intelligence is commonly known as personality, your "soft skills," character, or even communication skills. Emotional intelligence is one of the most important skills you can have. Research studies indicate that emotional intelligence is ten times more important for success than IQ and technical skills combined, especially when in leadership roles. Emotional intelligence is an individual's skill at perceiving, understanding, and managing emotions. Unlike your IQ, your emotional intelligence is a fluid skill that can be greatly improved through increased awareness and commitment to change. According to the research, emotional intelligence is more important than IQ and technical expertise combined. Some studies indicate that emotional intelligence is more than twice as important as standard IQ abilities. The other eighty percent of the factors are related to emotional intelligence. For some, it is a characteristic of people similar to intellectual ability or creativity, while others believe it is simply applying our intelligence to the emotional components of our lives. Emotional intelligence is an intelligent use of your emotions that is reflected in your behavior when responding, rather than reacting to situations. At work, emotional intelligence is important in teamwork. There are five domains of emotional intelligence: Knowing your emotions; managing your own emotions; motivating yourself; recognizing and understanding other people's emotions; and managing relationships or managing the emotions of others. As a facilitator, a team leader must have a high emotional intelligence, if the team is to perform at a high level. The high-emotional intelligence leader is able to rally team members with high emotional competence and harness EQ and other strengths to boost team performance. The workplace is changing and changing fast. Emotional competence can be grouped into personal competence and social competence. Personal competencies, like self-awareness, self-regulation and motivation, determine how we manage ourselves. Emotional awareness occurs when you recognize how various emotions shape what you perceive, think and do. Self-confidence is necessary for you to sustain superior performance. Without self-confidence, you lack the conviction essential for taking on tough challenges. Self-regulation would include managing your internal impulses and your ability to keep disruptive emotions in check. Emotional intelligence supports your motivation. Social competencies, such as empathy and social skills, determine how well you handle relationships. Empathy is essential as an emotional guidance system, helping us to get along well at work.

Emotional intelligence impacts every area of our life, health, learning, behavior and relationships. The issues of today's emerging diverse population relative to excellence and emotional intelligence represent a new area of research. Emotions are a resourceful mode of communication. Social intelligence is important for success in an environment where work is done in teams. It possible to assess how emotionally intelligent individuals are and then create best practice program interventions to improve their emotional intelligence in a targeted area, such as effective listening that bring about improvements and genuine changes. All emotional competencies can be cultivated with the right practice. Interpersonal intelligence is the ability to be sensitive to other people's emotions and psychological states. Interpersonal intelligence enables us to choose appropriate responses. Intrapersonal and interpersonal intelligence make up what we now call emotional intelligence. Daniel Goleman of Harvard wrote a book called "Emotional Intelligence: why it is as important as IQ" helped us to understand emotional intelligence and provided more clarity. Emotional intelligence indicates our ability for using that awareness to achieve positive outcomes.

Emotional intelligence is relevant because it provides you with a new way to understand and assess people's behaviors, management styles, attitudes, interpersonal skills, and potential. Emotional intelligence determines your potential for learning the practical skills that are based on EI's five elements or competencies: self-awareness, motivation, self-regulation, empathy, and adeptness in relationships. An emotional competence is a learned capability based on emotional intelligence that results in outstanding performance at work.

Your emotion influences everything you do. Emotional competencies determine and explains how you manage yourselves...social competencies determine how you handle relationships. Emotional Intelligence explains how effectively we reflect and respond to our emotions and relate to the emotions of others. Emotional Intelligence helps you to solve problems. The core competency underlying effective leadership skills is emotional intelligence. Emotional intelligence skills are very accurate in predicting performance and success in leaders. A key emotional intelligence component, self-awareness, is your ability to recognize and understand your moods, emotions and drives and in particular the impact these have on those around you in the work environment. In a Harvard Business Review article entitled "What Makes a Leader," study investigating the relationship between emotional intelligence and leadership, emotional intelligence was cited as a distinguishing factor in leadership performance. This included emotional competence dimensions in: Self-confidence, achievement orientation, initiative, leadership, influence and change catalyst. Interestingly, a Johnson & Johnson's Consumer Companies study found fewer emotional intelligence performance and potential dimensions differences relating to gender. In the Johnson study, women scored significantly higher on Empathy, Interpersonal Relationships, and Social Responsibility, while men scored higher on self-actualization, assertiveness, stress tolerance, impulse control, and adaptability. Emotional intelligence is lacking when, instead of accurate awareness, perceptions are marred by misconceptions.

Your emotional intelligence is a major factor in your career success and personal happiness. Emotional intelligence is a proven tool and a leading driver of success. Raising your emotional intelligence offers practical tips and suggestions for developing emotional intelligence and reaping its benefits in any situation or work environment. Emotional intelligence is self-awareness. Emotional intelligence is self and relationship management. It helps to improve productivity, accountability and bottom line performance. We should avoid "emotional hijacking" which contributes to derailing a professional's performance.

Emotional intelligence is the essential building block in the leaders' ability to establish the right climate for you to succeed as a leader. Leaders at all levels of the organization must demonstrate daily a high degree of emotional intelligence in their leadership roles. There is a direct link between emotional intelligence and leadership performance and it gives leaders specific ways to improve their performance. You can improve your emotional intelligence in the five components of emotional intelligence: your self-awareness, understanding other people, motivating yourself, controlling your emotions, and inspiring others. Rather than ignoring your emotions, you need to bring intelligence to emotions. If you want to improve your emotional intelligence, concentrate on building skills in knowing your emotions, regulating your emotions, applying self-control and self-discipline, cultivating empathy, managing relationships, striving for social competence and honing your leadership skills.

Principles

- Your excellence is the basis of your happiness and happiness is the reward of excellence.

- If you want to find your passion in life, look for work involving excellence in service to others and being connected to a greater good.

DREAM GREATNESS BE UNSTOPPABLE

3
THINK THE RIGHT THOUGHTS TO SUCCEED

"There is no obstacle in the path of young people who are poor or members of minority groups that hard work and preparation cannot cure."

— Barbara Jordan, Songs of Wisdom: Quotations from Famous African Americans 20th Century

Envision Your Future, Your Life Will Reflect What You Think

Success is difficult to define because it means different things to different people. It even means different things to the same people at different times. Success is a moving goal. It sometimes exists for a very long time, such as in a successful relationship, or it may last for only an instant, such as hitting the game-winning basket. Some people associate success with happiness. If we are happy we are certainly successful. It's easier to be successful when you're happy doing what you do. If we're not happy in our work, in order to enhance our chance for success we're going to have to change what we're doing, change where we're doing it, or change our attitude about what we are doing. We have known people who have changed jobs because they were unhappy, only to wind up being unhappy again but just in a different place. Changing our attitude is often overlooked.

Success comes from doing our absolute best, which is something only you can determine. To be successful we can't sit back and wait for things to happen, we have to make them happen. Success is unique to each person and our success should not be measured by comparing ourselves with others. Our success should be compared against our own potential, measured by the distance traveled and the obstacles we have had to overcome, not by where we are at any particular time.

Our thoughts can affect our behavior for success and enjoyment. Positive thinking is about change and focuses on achieving success that to date have been elusive in our personal or professional relationships, communication, and work. Positive thinking allows us to learn new skills quicker than before; overcome limiting self beliefs; manage ourselves and our emotions more effectively; achieve higher levels of concentration and focus; liberate ourselves from fears and phobias; re-connect with the fun and enjoyment. Each of us must find our own definitions for success and shoot for them. And always remember that a setback isn't a failure unless we quit.

Our thoughts that we recall about past experiences produce images that come back when we think of that event, any sounds that we heard and the strongest feelings that we felt return as a part of our memory and appears real. This is because our subconscious cannot tell the difference between reality and imagination. Our subconscious processes what our senses tell it and if we tell it warm, comforting clear things, then that's what we will experience. The same happens when we tell ourselves what we don't want to happen. For example "I know I am not going to succeed", "I don't want to get a promotion", or "I must not think negatively." All these are instructions to the subconscious to do exactly what it hears us thinking. Our subconscious cannot distinguish between verbal positives or negatives. Therefore it is better to say "I will win," or "I am a positive thinker." These statements not only reframe your thinking but are said as if you are already doing them. Therefore the brain perceives and acts on these new positive beliefs as if they are already in place. All these techniques can be learned and like other skills need to be practiced and provided guidance after the initial training. We can change our pattern of thinking from negative to positive using the power of positive words and verbal communication.

People who do not succeed in life are more receptive and have a susceptibility to being angry and bitter. A range of anger results in criminal behavior, juvenile delinquency, social and health problems and emotional malaise in our community. Low emotional illiteracy results in thinking before acting; failure and frustration; feeling of hopelessness; aggressive behavior; lashing out as a reaction; irrational thoughts and beliefs. Emotional illiteracy is an underlying cause of crime and overall lack of success. We have opportunities to reeducate ourselves in key areas such as: mastery of purpose and vision, self awareness and control, empathy, social expertness and personal influence. You can harness the untapped power of your emotions to enjoy success. The challenge is the mastery of your purpose and vision. Also, you must develop your self-awareness and control, empathy on the inside and social expertness and personal influence on the outside. We must be optimistic in the face of failure and frustration. We must be able to recover quickly from our perceived failures, anger and learn how to manage emotions with intelligence.

There is a universal law that says, if you form a picture in your mind of what you would like to be, and you keep and hold that picture there long enough, you will soon become exactly as you have been thinking. You are what you think. We have the power to envision our future, with courage even during troubled times. During difficult times, we need to be mindful that something great comes out of our trials and misfortune. Our deepest desires and dreams align with the essence of who we are. The more we align with that essence, the more our life holds meaning, purpose and fulfillment. Our desires and dreams provide us with a sense of our destiny. Our self image is made up of our experiences, desires and other people's ideas and expectations of us that often has little to do with who we really are.

Betrayals exist on all levels. Betrayal presents an opportunity to adjust our life to be more authentic. There are large betrayals such as the end of a relationship and small betrayals or disappointments.

The solution to many of our problem exist within each of us. Peace, joy, health and well-being can be found inside us. These solutions already exist within us, they are waiting to be discovered. Asking is the first step. Knowing yourself, gives us basis for thinking positively about step one. If you don't know who you are, you can get caught up in illusions: materialism, business, career, status, politics, religions, and other limitless and endless social illusions. If you know who you are and what you want, you will have a better chance of figuring out how to achieve success, happiness and personal fulfillment.

We all have values. We must make sure that the values we choose to define ourselves are our own values and not someone else's who may be defined them as right or wrong values from their perspective. If you value knowledge, structure a lifestyle where you are constantly learning. If you love being surrounded by beauty, open your eyes to the beauty all around you study art, literature, and sciences. Remember to choose something that you have a talent in. If family is important to you, family can mean many things. It can be people that you are related to or just a group of people that you are close to. Envision your future and choose a professional and personal life that is worthwhile to you.

To know yourself is to clarify your gifts, your talents, life challenges and how you experience your personality and soul. The first step is to find out what is behind our procrastination and then take time out to create discipline, to rest and discern their effect on our lives. We need to experience real "free time" and peace of mind by setting meaningful goals. We need to begin to better manage our time, stay on track and be more efficient getting more done more easily. The more we understand and know about who we are; we gain self appreciation, our levels of self-acceptance increases, while our negativity decreases along with many of our fears and anger. Our self esteem improves dramatically, our courage increases and we have increased hope and joy. If you have feelings of emptiness, feelings of meaningless and you want your life to have more purpose, remember, you're not alone. Just knowing your life's purpose and fully living it brings meaning and fulfillment. When we consciously align with our deepest reasons for being, we tap into our inner energy, personal power and passion. By doing this, our lives will flow in new and enjoyable ways.

Create a personal vision statement based on your choice. Identify the motivation, values, qualities and talents that influenced your decision. Joy, as the energy of love, is one of the highest goal we can have. According to the universal Law of Attraction, as we think and feel we vibrate. And as we vibrate, we attract. We need to simply bring the joy, love and happiness that are already inside us to life. Activate your joy, love and happiness and begin to experience ways to go beyond conditional happiness to the peaceful state of joy. Remember, as you resonate with joy, you automatically draw to you a more meaningful, healthy, loving life. Redefine success and what abundance means to you and draw on your passion to magnetize prosperity to you. Become conscious of what is now unconscious in you and your life will transform. Be yourself, be your best self and make a difference in your self and the world.

The Power of Thought

Positive affirmation is a good thing. It encourages us to excel and become everything we dreamed. We should never give up...success is on the way. The person with a positive expectation always goes for the prize. Positive thinking is the winner's edge, the extra push that brings the success we have been looking for.

It is crucial that we learn to think critically, problem solve and understand the power of our thoughts. Our thoughts play an important role in our life. Less talented people can often do the work of those with more talent and skills when they are transformed by the power of their thoughts and mental concentration. Successful people consider every possibility that makes an art of both work and life.

Pain or perceived pain also challenges our thinking and perception, which ultimately directs our life. If we want to get rid of pain, we must become more conscious of the causes of our pains. Our minds are very powerful. Intention supports efficiency with time management. Intention supports us in overcoming obstacles and problem-solving. Many of us realize that we do not need to be sick or hurt to take a vacation. We realize the power of thoughts on our daily manifestations. There is an old saying, "Our past thoughts have created our current reality, and we are creating our futures with the thoughts we have right now." Many of us believe that we create our own destiny using the power of our thoughts, positive thinking and creative visualization. Frequently repeated thoughts with concentration and desire eventually produce results. It is a proven fact that thoughts have power. Most people are unaware of this fact, though we constantly use this power and unconsciously attract circumstances and situations into our lives.

Successful people have learned techniques for creating and innovating with thoughts, using thought power in a conscious way. This means that your life is affected both by your thoughts and behavior and by others' too. Take into consideration, on the mental plane thoughts coalesce with other similar thoughts and gain more power. A group of people thinking about the same subject manifests more power then a single person. Similar thoughts strengthen each other, and opposite thoughts weaken each other. If you desire something, and all the people around are opposed, they can neutralize your power, unless your inner power is stronger than our collective inner powers.

Changes in your attitude can eventually transform your circumstances or situations. The energy of our thoughts move outward in wave patterns like a river. Since your thoughts move outward, all thoughts become woven and connected to other thoughts. Some call it the still voice. Communication can occur without words. It takes place through feelings, through knowing, through the eyes that reflect and radiate the essence of your soul reality, through gentle and sensitive movement of your body, through understanding transmitted from your inner voice. Communication is always taking place. Your future can be changed, and this change is guided by your thoughts. You can discover ways to use your inner power to create a vision for your perfect future. Your intention matters because of the energy it constantly pulls toward you. Your thoughts are critical to your success, and they matter. Notice the word matter. Our thoughts create matter. Thoughts control matter; therefore your intentions are a key ingredient in creating the life you deserve. Give something mundane an intention and its matter will change. So imagine what happens if you actually give it energy. Find a love source inside, bring it forth, and guide it toward higher thoughts.

Thought is life. Your thoughts create your environment. Your thoughts constitute your world, good or bad. Simply stated, if we entertain healthy thoughts, we can keep good health. If we hold on to sickly unhealthy thoughts in our mind, we can never expect good health, beauty and harmony in our life. Our body is the product of our mind. A thought is life and our thoughts are irreplaceable. Remember as the Soaps put it, "We only have but one life to live," and "these are the days of our lives."

As a reader, we read about suffering from time to time and are reminded that no one can escape suffering. The state of our body is a reflection of the state of our mind, so it is important that we cultivate our mental strengths to face life's adversity and be able to bravely face anything in life. The mind can influence overall health and disorders, including various immune system related diseases such as chronic disease and cancer can be tackled, to an extent, with the power of thought. If we allow our bodies to convince our minds of sickness, our suffering will double. If we neglect our body and do not strengthen our mind, we may acquire one or more chronic diseases. From another perspective abundance is a state of mind. We create it with our thoughts. Our thoughts have a power of their own. If we can understand and utilize that power, we can accomplish a lot more in our lives. Our thoughts and our state of being go hand in hand and together they create the experience we call life. Positive thoughts create a positive life, bringing us its rich rewards. Negative thoughts do the same thing in a negative way. Begin today to understanding the power of your thoughts and cultivate the habit of letting your mind gain control.

Thinking for a Change...Commit to Happiness

Like many of you, I have read numerous inspirational articles and books and heard a variety of positive thinking audio tapes. Self awareness is being aware of your consciousness and inner thoughts but also include understanding that other people are self-aware. Spiritually, our consciousness can extend through time and space as far as we intend. When we apply consciousness, we are viewing, we are simply aware. There is a difference between consciousness and perception. If we extend our consciousness to a specific area, we can occupy with that consciousness the exact space we choose depending on the size of the playing field we require. Once we have this consciousness, we are able to apply our perception. If we need to perceive across a number of areas to play a game, we simply extend our consciousness further. If a situation calls for only limited perception, our consciousness can be reduced. Consciousness and perception work hand in hand and with thought and reflection; we can increase our skill in using both.

We can restrict ourselves by viewing events in our life from one consciousness. It starts at an early age when we begin to replace our own consciousness with the consciousness of others. Consciousness is our inner being, our awareness, perception and realization. Developing the power of concentration, practicing meditation and trying to be aware of our consciousness is the key that opens the door of understanding.

Dissatisfaction seems to be a part of life, even if we are seeking happiness and even if we manage to find temporary happiness. Success people think different from unsuccessful people. To achieve their personal and professional potential, successful people are disciplined, reflective, creative, unselfish and understand the big-picture and able to break down complex issues with strategic thinking. Successful people have these things in common. Unsuccessful people tend not to be disciplined and don't see the big picture

Changing from negative to positive thinking isn't always easy, especially if you have a difficult time with change. For some people, change is a life-long struggle. I am reminded that our life today is a result of our thinking yesterday. Do you know what most people's second challenge is when it comes to making positive personal changes? It's their feelings. They want to change, but they don't know how to get past their emotions. But there is a way to do it. You can begin with the following two premises: Major Premise: I can control my thoughts. Minor Premise: My feelings come from my thoughts. Conclusion: I can control my feelings by controlling my thoughts.

If you are willing to change your thinking, you can change your feelings. If you change your feelings, you can change your actions. And changing your actions based on good thinking can change your life.

Where success is concerned, people are not measured in inches or pounds or college degrees or family background; they are measured by the size of their thinking. Good thinking will improve your life. Good thinking is important. As I was taught, good thoughts and actions can never produce bad results; bad thoughts and actions can never produce good results. It may seem obvious that the quality of people's thinking leads to the quality of their results. Most people agree with that fact. Poor thinking produces negative progress. Average thinking produces no progress. Good thinking produces some progress. Great thinking produces great progress.

Some people expect to change their results without changing their thinking. The greatest detriment to many people's success tomorrow is your thinking today. If your thinking is limited, so is your potential. But if you keep growing in your thinking, you will continually outgrow what you're doing. The good news is that no matter how complicated life gets or how difficult problems may seem, good thinking can make a difference, if you make it a consistent part of your life. Achievement comes from the habit of good thinking. Sadly, we don't all know this, unsuccessful people focus their thinking on survival, while average people focus their thinking on maintenance and successful people focus their thinking on progress.

A change in your thinking can help you to move from survival or maintenance to real progress. Good thinking isn't just one thing. It consists of several specific thinking skills. For good thinking, you need all the thinking "pieces" to become the kind of person who can achieve great things.

- We need to begin to see the wisdom of big-picture thinking. We need to unleash the potential of focused thinking.
- We need to discover the joy of creative thinking.
- We need to recognize the importance of realistic thinking.
- We need to release the power of strategic thinking. We need to feel the energy of possibility thinking.
- We need to embrace the lessons of reflective thinking. We need to question the acceptance of popular thinking. We need to encourage the participation of shared thinking.
- We need to experience the satisfaction of unselfish thinking. We need to enjoy the return of bottom-line thinking.

As you become acquainted with each skill, you will find that some people do well, others people don't. We need to master all that we can, including the process of shared thinking which helps us compensate for our weak areas, and our life will change. It can revolutionize your life.

Emotional and Rational Thinking

No matter how progressive and politically correct you have become, people still tend to believe that when making decisions, men are less driven by emotions than women. Research says, men use left-brained logical, rational thinking and women have more emotional intuitive (sensitive) skills. In reality, both men and women make decisions emotionally. We learn emotionally. Our social skills and Likability are based on emotions. People don't choose rationally to listen to your message and then have a feeling about it. You use logical or rational thinking to determine if the decision is worth it.

Thinking isn't always verbal. Critical thinking is not passively taking in information. Some people are intuitive, they are insightful and in tuned with their emotions. Intuitive people stand out because of their keen observations, quick minds and ability in choosing the best solutions. Intuition is clearly related to emotional intelligence.

You may believe your emotions are automatic reactions to events, events happen and trigger emotions, and that is all there is to it. Most people make decisions with their hearts and then use logic or rational thinking to confirm them. Nothing can destroy logic and rational thinking faster than emotion. Emotional intelligence is about managing emotion. Emotional reactions are split into two groups: unhealthy and healthy. Unhealthy emotions such as depression, anger, anxiety, guilt, involve the individual in focusing on the emotional upset rather than on the problem; excessive introspection can mean valuable time wasted. Unhealthy emotions are largely determined by irrational beliefs. Healthy emotions are largely determined by rational beliefs. By discussing emotional consequences, this indicates to individuals that thinking and feeling are equally important.

You tend to remain upset by continually indoctrinating yourselves with these irrational beliefs. We tend to live our lives unconsciously by habit. These habits keep us stuck in patterns that limit our experience of life. With awareness of our emotions and behaviors comes choice. And with choice, we exercise rational thinking.

Irrational thinking involves illogical ways of evaluating ourselves, others, and the world around us. Irrational thinking blocks us from achieving our goals and purposes. It creates extreme, persistent emotions that can distress and immobilize. Irrational thinking leads to behaviors that harm yourself, others and your life in general. Rational thinking is based in reality. Rational thinking helps you achieve your goals and purposes. It creates manageable emotions.

Rational thinking helps people to behave in ways which promote their goals. It should not be confused for positive thinking. Rational thinking is realistic thinking. It is concerned with facts, the real world, rather than subjective opinion or wishful thinking. Realistic thinking leads to realistic emotions. Realistic thinking avoids exaggeration of both kinds, negative and positive.

When under stress, we tend to think emotionally. Our brain works primarily through emotional pattern matching in the limbic systemlimbic system or emotional brain. Emotional thinking is very clear cut, black and white, all or nothing. Rational thinking is a function of the part of your brain called the neocortex. Critical thinking is the learnable skill that sorts 'real' information from the noise of what you are observing. This, along with other negative thinking, can cause intense stress and unhappiness and can severely damages self-confidence.

Negative thinking damages performance by undermining your self-confidence. You can counter negative thinking effectively so that you can perform at your best. Negative thinking can damage confidence, harm performance and paralyze mental skills. Thought awareness is the process by which you observe your thoughts and become aware of what is going through your head. There is no need to suppress any thoughts that you have. Thought awareness is the first step in the process of eliminating negative thoughts.

The next step in dealing with negative thinking is to challenge the negative thoughts that you wrote down using the Thought Awareness technique. Begin by writing your thoughts down, review every thought you wrote and rationally challenge them. Ask yourself whether the thought is reasonable. This, along with other negative thinking, can elevate your stress and unhappiness and severely undermine your self-confidence.

Negative thinking harms performance and paralyzes your mental skills. By logging or writing your negative thoughts for a reasonable period of time, you will quickly see patterns in your negative thinking. Thought awareness is the first step in the process of managing negative thoughts,. You cannot manage thoughts that you are unaware of.
You can choose to challenge your negative thoughts. If you perform as well as you reasonably can, then fair people are likely to respond fairly. If people are unfair, then this is something outside your control.

Awareness helps you to understand your negative thinking, unpleasant memories and misinterpretation of situations that may interfere with your performance. Rational thinking is the technique that helps you to challenge your negative thoughts and either learn from them or refute them as incorrect. Positive thinking is then used to create affirmations to counter your negative thoughts. These affirmations neutralize negative thoughts and build your self-confidence.

Multi-tasking Affects Ability to Think

The ability to multi-task is a powerful and wonderful capacity of your brain. In primitive times, it gave early men and women the capacity to hunt, gather, cook and keep track of the children at the same time. Today, it allows you to carry on a conversation while crossing the road and watching for traffic, to talk on your cell phone and chop vegetables without losing a finger. We listen to music while reading. Multi-tasking is a huge gift but recent research highlight potential dangers. Multi-tasking adversely affects how you learn. When you multi-task you are distracted while learning, but you are activating a different system in the brain than if you were to focus on a single task. When distracted, learning is less flexible and there is less understanding of new material. Multi-tasking hampers our ability to learn and retain things over the long term. In addition to learning, there has also been extensive research on the time-cost of multi-tasking. While we believe that we are getting more done in less time by balancing three things at once, research tells another story.

Multitasking works itself into interpersonal communication. Multitasking require more mental manipulation, discerning similarities and inconsistencies, drawing inferences, grasping new concepts and so on. Research shows that the quality of our output and depth of our thought deteriorates as we do more and more things at the same time, multitasking. It may seem that writing an instant message, burning a CD and talking to a friend about our weekend, are being done all at the same time but what's really going on is a rapid toggling among tasks rather than simultaneous processing. We're doing more than one thing, but we're ordering them and deciding which one to do at any one time. Multitasking does not allow us to rest, have needed mental downtime. We need to relax, have time when our mind is not focused on a task. The anterior prefrontal cortex of mind is used for multitasking. It helps you switch from one thing to the next thing then back to the first thing again. It is one of the first areas in our head to develop and one of the first to deteriorate as we age. In other words youth and folks over sixty don't multitask as well as the young adult.

When we try to do two or more related tasks at the same time or go back and forth quickly between them errors go way up and it takes longer often twice as long. The reality is we can't simultaneously be thinking about something and do something else or do two things at once. Many of us brag about being able to multitask but we will never ever be able to overcome the brain's limitations for processing information.

Consistent multitasking may even result in a condition that our brain gets so overexcited that we can't focus even if we wanted to. Eventually, you will lose that skill and your will not be able to concentrate. When we are toiling away at our jobs, trying to make a living and dealing with all the other demands on our time, we may brag about multitasking. As we multitask, we are trying to fit in more activities, than there are hours in the day. With no real quality time left, we still need to make sure we are not missing out on the intimacy of personal relationships which are critical to our overall health and wellness.

Multitasking makes us unintelligent. Imagine…typing this while talking on you cell phone to one person and instant messaging another. Try talking to one person on your cell phone and ordering lunch at the same time. Are we fooling ourselves that we can actually do these all these things without a loss of quality? Yes, we are. We need to understand that multitasking comes with a steep price tag. Many of us once believed that the myth of multitasking was about time, that doing four things simultaneously less time than to do those same four things in sequence. Scientists now know the myth is about quality. And it gets worse… it's not just quality that suffer, but your ability to think and learn may suffer as well. Some researchers believe that all this constant, warp speed; always-on multitasking is causing an inability to follow any topic deeply. Perhaps the biggest problem of all is that the majority of people doing the most multitasking are blind to how bad they are at it.

We believe we can e-mail and talk on the phone at the same time, with little or no degradation of either communication. We believe we can do homework while watching a movie, surf the web while talking to a friend/love one/colleague. But we can't, not without a hit on every level-- time, quality, and the ability to think deeply.

Whenever I talk about the big myth of multitasking, some people always tell me how they have the kind of brain that can do this. I just say right. They don't and even neither do I. None of us do. And maybe we'd realize that if we turn off our cell phone, disable IM, mute the little "ding" that says we've got email, and just sit there for a few moments. The big problem for most young people, it seems, is that they don't know how to "just sit there." They get the shakes after just a few minutes without media stimulation. Decades of research and plain old common sense indicate that the quality of one's output and depth of thought deteriorates as the number of tasks increases. I am often reminded of the saying "If you can spend a perfectly useless afternoon in a perfectly useless manner, you have learned how to live." I could not agree more.

Mind Over Matter – Think and Succeed

Norman Vincent Peale provides a guide to everyday living by urging readers to eliminate all the negative thoughts that prevent them from achieving happiness and success. I agree with Dr. Peale, you can learn to eliminate that demoralizing stumbling block, self doubt. You can free yourself from worry, stress, resentment, and move beyond your problems by visualizing solutions and then attaining them. Faith in yourself makes good things happen to you. Improved self-esteem and success will break your habit of worrying. Positive thinking will ensure you believe in yourself and everything you do, and develop the power to reach your goals. To improve your performance, think about outcomes such as targets or goals is a good idea. Success can be achieved by anyone. Anyone can achieve their dreams. No more switching to the latest DVD or fad diet, you can develop positive thinking ideas and concepts that can be followed for the rest of your life. There is a whole branch of medicine called psycho-neuro-immunology, which studies the effect of thoughts and emotions on our biochemistry. Health providers have known that psychological factors such as expectations play a role in the perception and experience of pain. People who work in pain clinics use cognitive therapy to help people manage their pain better. Research shows that by merely expecting pain to be less it will be less. Positive thinking may be as powerful as a shot of morphine for relieving pain and reducing both sensory and emotional processing activity of pain in parts of the brain that process pain information. If the ideas of easily rising to the top of your organization, succeeding in business or becoming wealthy sounds good to you, then you're going to love this book.

That's because *Dream Greatness Be Unstoppable* revels what successful people are secretly doing behind the scenes to make millions. They are using a universal concept, thinking to succeed. It doesn't have anything to do with intelligence. Yet, it takes time to put the concept "Thinking to Succeed" into action and then be on your way to accomplishing your life dreams. Do you hate your job or the current business you're in? The fact of the matter is, you can finally move beyond the 9-to-5 rat race. Imagine not working for a boss who doesn't truly value you! You can tell your boss to shove it. When Sunday evening rolls around, you won't be stressing out about waking up early Monday morning to make the dashboard-pounding drive to work. Instead, you'll relax and enjoy your evening all the more. You can make it a party. You can do that when you have this lifestyle. If you want to succeed, you'll need to finish reading this book right away.

We are thinking negatively when we fear the future, put ourselves down, criticize ourselves for errors, doubt our abilities, or expect failure. Negative thinking damages our confidence, harms our performance and paralyzes our mental skills. You have the capacity to change and to adopt a new beliefs and conviction whenever the chance arises. We also have the ability to create that chance. Our thoughts create an irresistible appeal around us that attracts certain energies, which then causes the formation of certain conditions for change. By replacing old, negative thought patterns with positive, faith-filled energy, our lives will change for the better. Once again, we will have created exactly what we've been thinking about, mind over matter. Mind and thought awareness is the process by which we observe our thoughts and become aware of what is going through our head.

If you find it difficult to look at your negative thoughts objectively, imagine that you are your best friend or a respected coach or mentor. Look at the list of your negative thoughts and imagine they were written by someone who asked you for advice. How you would challenge these thoughts? You can challenge negative thinking. You should be able to quickly see whether your thoughts are wrong, or whether they have some substance to them. Where there is substance to your negative thoughts, take appropriate action. In these cases, your negative thinking was an early warning system for you, showing where you need to direct your attention.

Positive affirmations help you to build self-confidence and change negative behavior patterns into positive ones. By basing your affirmations on the clear, rational assessments of fact that you made using rational thinking, you can undo the damage that negative thinking may have done to your self-confidence. According to the principles of neuro-linguistic programming, people receive and take in information by sight (visually), hearing (aurally) or by emotion (feeling). The key to establishing rapport lies in synchronizing behavior or mimicking the other person's pose, facial expression, gestures, body language and tone of voice.

Empowering Thought and Happiness

Don't you find it odd that happiness is something everyone wants, but we never ask for it. We were never taught how to get it, but they spend our whole life looking for it. Imagine how much easier life would be if there was an instruction book for reaching happiness. Happiness requires finding the right formula to get you in alignment by focusing on what is important to your outcomes. We can start by simply thinking and focusing and that will change our perspective or experience of the world. Imagine driving to work. You are thinking about a project or upcoming meeting, you are focused on specific aspects of what is challenging or going wrong with the project. With this new insight you can look at your project from a new perspective. You can see that the challenges have been created by your attention to them by implementing the step by step concepts of focusing you can make immediate changes in the outcome of the project you are working on. Who says you can't be happy all the time? Most people work hard without much direction, living between the hope of abundance and the fear of not having happiness. We lack direction in building a happy life for ourselves and our loved ones. Happiness should be the reason for almost every action we take. Unfortunately, happiness often requires that we do many things we'd rather not be doing, and in the process, we end up suffering from excessive stress. To prevent this from happening in the future, we must use our limited energy, time, and money wisely, in hope of finding genuine lasting happiness. Since happiness seems so elusive, we may have to coax it out and when we get to happiness, to prevent it from slipping away. There are over a billion people in the world who aren't as happy as they would like to be or could be and it has nothing to do with poverty or living in third-world conditions. It has to do with the way we think.

Do you remember your parents teaching you the methods for creating happiness? What about all those hours your teachers spent teaching you the precise actions needed to become happy? It is likely no one else remembers either. Sadly our education was meant to give us tools for living well, yet no one taught us happiness skills. Most people have spent years in school studying subjects that they have never used, yet not much time, if, any has been spent learning the methods for creating your happiness. Creating happiness is a skill we could use every day of our lives but it isn't even taught! What a tragedy!

As a result, so many people are just muddling through, learning by trial and error, lots and lots of errors. We have also learned many myths about happiness from peers, customs, advertising, and clever quotations...almost all of it worthless hearsay. Advertisers, for example, would have you buy every single product with their solemn promise that each one will bring you greater happiness. They show you smiling people as a result of time savings, cost reduction, excitement, sex, greedy consumption, rainbows, sunshine...all the usual tricks. Deep down in your heart, you know that it is an illusion but you consume anyway. People have been disappointed so often that they've become skeptical of almost any claim and they should be!

For most of us, the pursuit of happiness is our ultimate goal, it gives us hope and a reason for living. The search for happiness motivates us to go on in spite circumstances or setbacks. Happiness does not come from having material things. Overcoming unhappiness is a process of gaining knowledge of self and attaining satisfaction and happiness. Happiness is the state of being which follows the state of satisfaction in the growth of self. Happiness is common and it includes our sight, hearing, taste, touch, smell, feeling, thought, consciousness, memory and experience of satisfaction. We seek knowledge to realize our goal, happiness. Happiness comes from our knowledge. Happiness is knowledge which enables us to overcome unhappiness, maintaining a positive state of mind and lead a satisfying life. Happiness is knowledge. However, there is such a thing as "happiness knowledge," a very special kind of knowledge that tells us exactly how to create real lasting happiness. Happiness knowledge doesn't have all the glitz and glamour of those glossy advertisements. It is a quiet knowledge that has no need of gimmicks. It won't dazzle your eyes or hypnotize your senses. It won't delude you into believing that you'll become happier when you own Product X. Happiness knowledge deals with very simple things: How we can think in certain ways, and act in certain ways to cause the natural core of our being to light up. You know what I'm talking about because you've probably experienced it. Remember the times you knew deep feelings of satisfaction and contentment, the pride of newly-acquired skills, the warm glow of touching another soul through your kindness, the feeling of honorability when you did the right thing, the peacefulness of being in nature, or the sheer joy of doing what you love? This is happiness knowledge.

That said, there is a method to be continually happy. There's actually a whole collection of special physical and mental actions that we can use naturally and automatically to produce feelings of well-being. These actions are called happiness actions. Based on my research, I have written hundreds of articles about happiness actions and life-changing knowledge. Happiness is a way of living, not something that happens to you. No matter what your circumstances, no matter how hard you think things are, no matter your education or your upbringing, happiness actions can be applied to your life effectively. Here's an example, imagine you're going merrily along in life when suddenly you get a severe back injury that lands you in bed 22 hours a day. Days turn into weeks, weeks into months, and months into years. You undergo seven spine surgeries and are still having serious trouble. In the process, you lose your income and career. You can't drive, or even walk very far. Your savings drain away. You have to sell your car, and you rack up enormous debt. What do you think? Could you be happy going through this? It's hard to believe anyone could be. Now imagine this happening to a person who knew a large collection of happiness actions and used them throughout the ordeal. The result...this person actually became happier than he was before his injury. No, this person has not lost touch with reality. Far from it, this person used the happiness actions he or she learned as a child, from a wise elder. Those happiness actions were so ingrained, so automatic that it didn't even occur to them that they should be unhappy. Imagine that. Well, what you imagined was a real story. It happened to one of my friends! At the time, he didn't have the foggiest clue that anyone else would be unhappy in the same situation until he was asked, "How is it that you're still so happy?"

Although many people still believe the myth that happiness is a result of your circumstances and that your good luck controls your happiness. Happiness is almost never a result of your circumstances. We all have a gift, the highest gift anyone could have the ability to create our own happiness. Once you understand it, you won't get hung up in the many traps that stall people's lives for years. This gift is explicitly not a cure for depression, but practicing living a life of happiness will likely make you feel a whole lot better. Happiness education is the best education you can get or give to someone. Happiness creation is the most important day-to-day skill you can learn, and it's imperative that you share it with people in your life. Fortunately, it's also easily affordable, so there's no reason to live a lesser life. Happiness training involves life-changing lessons and lasts a lifetime. Unlike meditation or affirmations, happiness actions require no extra time. Instead, they're a different way of doing your regular activities, with happiness as a byproduct. To find happiness, we must know that happiness is a philosophy. Our beliefs relate to our happiness and happiness comes only when we know the right way to use our beliefs. Beliefs are in our environment and we need our belief to build a happy foundation. There are always opportunities for us to live abundantly by creating our own life-changing opportunities. We must have a positive attitude and not allow anything to destroy our happiness. We must focus and use the hidden microscopes and telescopes use by happy people. We must have goals which are about creating our meaningful life paths which are the critical ingredients of happy accomplishment. We must understand failure from the inside and learn how to extract happiness from failure by knowing what to do next. We must accentuate our positives realizing that our happiness is a journey which is predictable when we see it wisely. We must develop awareness and use our awareness to enhance the spirit of our lives. We must understand that there is a positive side of stress and fall in love with that kind of stress, but not the way we think.

Thought is powerful and is our powerhouse. Our thoughts and our thinking will evolve us to your happiness. We have both the freedom and creativity, now it is time to tap into our ultimate freedom by removing all our fears by stealing its power. Thinking is play and play is fun, so we should have fun on our way to happiness. All too often we can't find the words to express our feelings or emotions at the time, so then we refer back to hostile terms or profanity and make profane statements. We must choose the words we use carefully and listen to what we say. We must then use happiness words and listen to what we say so that our actions will follow each part of our brain to create happiness. We must create a thought environment and multiply our brain power. We must begin to live a spiritual life of quality and achieve the greatest happiness which changes everything.

We are often reminded that true and lasting happiness always comes from within. We must create joy in our life and work. This is our life and not a dress rehearsal. We must be inspired to dream bigger and live out our dreams. People often refer to luck. Real luck is much more than mere chance. It's a way of using our awareness to attract things, events and people into our life. That's the secret. Now you know the secrets that can make anyone "lucky." Live cheerfully almost every waking moment by making small but simple adjustments in your beliefs, your outlook, and your action, so that people will turn to you smiling and say, "How did you get to be so lucky?" The 'happiness actions' are obvious once you know them, but not at all obvious to most people who suffer on the path of stress and conflict.

Principles

- Happiness is a thought, a feeling of contentment, even peacefulness that rarely arrives without a struggle.

- Success follows your thoughts when you are doing what you always wanted to do.

DREAM GREATNESS BE UNSTOPPABLE

4
LIKABILITY, MAGNETISM AND SUCCESS

"Bringing the gifts that my ancestors gave, I am the dream and the hope of the slave. I rise I rise I rise."

— Maya Angelou, *"Still I Rise, And Still I Rise"*

Likability as the First Impression

Likability is really important to any aspect of success. Communicating effectively professionally and personally is a key to success. Just imagine, within the first three seconds of a new encounter, we are evaluated. People appraise our visual and behavioral appearance from head to toe. They observe our demeanor, mannerisms, and body language, assess our grooming and accessories, watch, handbag, briefcase. In the business world, nothing can have a greater negative impact than a bad first impression. Client relations or customer service is a difficult term to define or measure because people tend to have different standards for it. No matter what definition is chosen, the most important component of quality client or customer service is the all-important first impression.

Within those fifteen seconds, we make an indelible impression. We may intrigue some and disenchant others. This first impression process occurs in every new situation. Within the first few seconds, people pass judgment on you, looking for common surface clues. Once the first impression is made, it is virtually irreversible. The process works like this:

- If you appear to be of comparable business or social level, you are considered suitable for further interaction.

- If you appear to be of higher business or social status, you are admired and cultivated as a valuable contact.

- If you appear to be of lower business or social standing, you are tolerated but kept at arm's length.

- If you are in an interview situation, you can either appear to match the corporate culture or not, ultimately affecting the outcome.

It is human nature to constantly make appraisals of people in business and social environments. We may hardly have said a word, but once this three-second evaluation is over, the content of our speech will not change it. When we make the best possible first impression, we have our audience in the palm of our hand. When we make a poor first impression, we lose our audience's attention, no matter how hard we try to recover it.

A positive first impression opens many opportunities. A negative first impression is hard to overcome and is an additional impediment to developing a relationship. We all like to be liked, valued, listened to, respected, trusted, and cared for. A positive first impression can help clients or customers feel all of those and more. A negative first impression means your efforts to build trust; rapport and loyalty will be more difficult. There's something memorable about a person who seems happy, enthusiastic, and motivated. We can learn to make a positive and lasting first impression, by modifying it to suit any situation, and we will come out a winner. Doing so, will require us to assess and identify our personality, physical appearance, lifestyle, and goals. Those who do will have the advantage. Success comes to those with integrity, those that are resourceful, and those that make a fabulous impression.

Every person has a "Likability-factor," an indicator of how likeable you are. Likeable people are friendly, communicative, open and connect with others. They are seen as trustworthy, motivated and hard-working, and are more likely to succeed in the workplace as well as inspire performance in others. Those with a low Likability factor, on the other hand, are perceived as arrogant and manipulative, tend to be unfriendly, quick to anger and hold grudges against others. No matter how likeable you think you are, there is always room for improvement.

Likability Supports Relationship-Building

We are consistently attracting. Every single thing you have in your life right now, you're either in resonance with it or, if it's not in your life, you're not in resonance with it. If you want to create anything you want, anything you desire, you have to practice three things, thoughts feeling and actions. Your thoughts, your feelings, and your actions all need to working together at the same time and in alignment. When you go three for three, you're absolutely unstoppable. You can create anything you want. The law of attraction says "like attracts like." So, if you want to be successful you need to come from a place of vibrating that you're successful. You need to be thinking about the successes you already have. For example, if you want to attract more money you need to be thinking abundantly, even though you might only be making $20,000 a year you want to be focusing on your gratitude for that coming from a state of abundance. If you're talking all the time about what you don't want or how bad it is, then what you're going to attract is more how bad it is.

Your life is a popularity contest, whether or not you want to admit it. If you don't generate positive emotional experiences, you will lose. If you take two equally talented people in any field, the one who is more likeable and better at connecting to people will be more successful life. Success is about Likability. I discovered that when you possess Likability, your success, your health, and your personal happiness increases because people are attracted to you feeling you will bring out the best in them. Your Likability influences what people believe, what people listen to, and what people value.

I have found that that your Likability is your capacity to produce positive emotional experiences in other people; that is what makes you likeable. The reason a person likes you is that you put a smile on their face. Likability is the capacity to deliver strong psychological benefits. If you flip it around, un-likeable people have the capacity to instill negative emotional experiences in people. Un-likeable people deliver psychological costs, not benefits. A likeable person is an emotional savior, a breath of fresh air, a lift. An un-likeable person is a challenge. Being likeable is not about being agreeable. It's not about being fake or phony or giving false praise or mirroring somebody else's moods or using their name hundreds of times in a sentence. These are all ways to try to create a positive emotional experience. Fundamentally, Likability is developing these core capabilities to generate positive emotional experiences; the capabilities that I focus on in this book. I consider friendliness, relevance in connecting with interests or needs, empathy and authenticity admirable qualities for anyone to posse.

Tim Sanders author of "The Likability Factor: How to Boost Your L-Factor and Achieve Your Life's Dreams" cites the power of Likability. I agree with Sanders, if we want to succeed in any endeavor, you must first be liked. People who are well liked are more apt to get what they want out of life than those who are disliked. Emotional intelligence personality traits such as friendliness, relevance in connecting with interests or needs, empathy and genuine authenticity contribute to your Likability. The more you are liked or the higher your Likability factor, the higher your success potential and the happier your life will be.

Are you wondering how you can improve your relationships with your friends and family? Are you curious how to get or keep the job of your dreams? Do you want to become a more popular person? Well, it is possible to learn how to do all that by raising your Likability factor that is the degree to which other people like you. After all, life is a series of popularity contests. The choices other people make about you contribute how you feel about your health, wealth, and happiness. And decades of research prove that people choose who they like. They vote for them, they buy from them, they marry them, and they spend precious time with them.

Likable can be critical. A number of studies indicated that likable employees are favored by co-workers; employees don't want to work with someone they disliked regardless to how skilled he or she is. Organizations have traditionally focused on competencies and thinking ability for hiring. There is growing recognition, however, that job effectiveness can be undone if an employee is disliked. Being proficient at job tasks is of little comfort to the organization if an employee's lack of friendliness alienates clients or other staff. Likability can also influence customers. Customers' perceptions of the employees they deal with can influence their overall feelings toward the organization they represent. Personality counts. It can mitigate mistakes, and help career advancement. Likable employees are more likely to get bigger pay raises and promotions. Employees with skills in relationship-building are often seen as valuable to an organization. Many people believe that their pleasant personalities have helped them to get ahead.

Co-workers who work with a likable colleague are more comfortable and tend to be more collaborative. Some employers stress hiring likable employees. In other words, employers may not hire someone they think may have an attitude. The bottom line is, it is not worth hiring someone you dislike, or someone who is likely to be disliked by other employees. Likability serves as a public relations tool in developing and nurturing relationships in any profession. To the extent that interpersonal skills are linked to relationship building, the value of Likability is even more pronounced.

The good news is that you can develop and enhance your Likability. You can win life's battles for preference. Our individual so-called Likability "intangibles" typically refer to such things as chemistry, fit, personality and presence. For example, when we speak favorably of your chemistry, fit, or personality, we generally mean that you interact comfortably with others, and have the ability to effectively "manage" equally well. We also generally mean you are deemed to be a valuable team member and integrates smoothly into organizational networks and cultures.

Likability starts with your conversation. Your first impression helps to build a relationship over time. The difference between a relationship conducted on the run and a relationship that will create loyalty and long-term business is comparable to the difference between a long-term, loving relationship and a one-night stand. Likeable people demonstrate a level of intimacy that reveals their unique ability to quickly forge the kind of emotional connection that builds trust, followed by lots of business. Likability makes others feel important and creates an environment where a person is not afraid to open up and show vulnerability. The more you are liked or the higher your Likability factor, the happier your life will be.

You can raise or improve your Likability factor by enhancing your personality. This includes:

- Being aware of how people react to you and them, and what you need to change to make people feel warmer toward you.

- Being friendly by eliminating unfriendliness from your behavior.

- Being relevant by communicating and connecting with others so they want to relate to you.

- Being understanding other peoples' passions.

- Being empathetic by listening and respecting other people's feelings.

- Being real and enthusiastic.

You can become wiser and wittier using Likability as a tool. You can achieve amazing positive outcomes.

Building Self-Awareness to Influence Others

In life, influence is a key skill. Self-awareness and influence helps you to earn cooperation, ensures that your voice is heard and makes you a better leader. Everyone has a degree of influence on some activity every day, without knowing it. The real skill is learning how to influence through commitment, loyalty and trust, rather than through mere compliance or, at worst, pressure. Making things happen in organizations depends on influencing sideways and upwards as much as it does on managing through the hierarchy. Organization change processes are best achieved through influence rather than imposition. We must be clear in our mind about the end result we want to achieve. Then we must identify the key stakeholders who we need to influence, get to know their needs and their perspective. Understanding the motivation, priorities and concerns of those you are trying to influence will help you connect with them and build influential relationships.

You need a heightened sense of self-awareness. For example are you a strategic visionary, down-to-earth pragmatist, head-led, analytical, sensitive, creative, risk-taker, or safe-bet decision-maker type? In building your self-awareness and influence imagine that you are the following:

- You are optimistic and you expect the best in this best of all possible worlds. You have an optimistic mood; optimistic plans and you take an optimistic view.

- You are passionate. You are capable of having powerful emotions. You have a passionate personality, temperament, and strong desire. You speak out against injustice.

- You are peaceful. You are tranquil and appear to be undisturbed by strife, turmoil, or disagreement. You are calm and inclined to peace and being peaceable. You believe peace is possible if make peace a part of their happiness which can be shared.

- You are positive. You display certainty, acceptance and a positive affirmation as you move forward on your journey. You appear determined, and confident but not arrogant. You are concerned with practical rather than theoretical matters.

- You are a highly respected and feeling person. Your emotional and physical responses are appropriate and effective. Our feelings are natural. We are not able to stop them from happening. But you act responsibly towards your feelings, in both words and actions; you have learned to respect yourself and others.

- You are skilled in developing others. You have the ability to foster the long-term learning or development of others. You focus is on the developmental intent and effect rather than on the formal role of teaching or training. You spend time helping people find their own way to excellence through specific feedback on current performance. You offer feedback to improve another person's performance. You mentors or coaches others. You recognize specific strengths of others. You provide inspirational leadership. You have the ability to take on the role as leader of a team or group. You have a desire to lead others. Your leadership is generally, but not always, shown from a position of formal authority. You work to bring people together to get the job done.

- You are able to build a strong sense of belonging within the group, leading others to feel they are part of something larger than themselves. You make activities or projects engaging. You inspire others by articulating a vision or a mission. You motivate others by arousing emotions. You influence. You have the ability to persuade, convince, or impact others in order to get them to go along with or support your agenda.

- You are able to grab someone's attention and impart something they want to hear. You know how to make others stand up and listen. You build consensus and support for positions. You convince others by appealing to their self-interest. You anticipate how people will respond to an argument and adapt your approach accordingly. You communicate. You send clear and convincing messages to an audience in an open and effective way. You make your presentations in an engaging style and are open to dialogue with the audience. You use an engaging presentation style. You use nonverbal cues, like tone of voice, to express feelings that reinforce messages in presentations. You use examples or visual aids to clarify or underscore messages when making a presentation.

- You are a change catalyst. You have the ability to alert, energize, and lead groups to bring about specific changes in the way things are done. You recognize the need for change and taking ownership of change initiatives in order to move the group or department forward. You remove barriers to change. You personally lead change initiatives. You call attention to the need for change.

- You are a skilled in conflict resolution. You handle difficult individuals, groups of people, or tense situations with diplomacy and tact. You come face-to-face with the conflict rather than trying to avoid it. You focus on the issues rather than the people and working to de-escalate the bad feelings. You bring disagreements out in the open. You help de-escalate conflicts. You communicate the positions of those involved in a conflict to all concerned. You build bonds. You work to build or maintain friendly, reciprocal, and warm relationships or networks of contacts with people. You build Bonds by developing and maintaining good relationships with a variety of people. You make close personal friends with acquaintances or classmates. You have a wide, informal network of colleagues. You nurture relationships related to activities or projects.

- You are a facilitator of teamwork and collaboration. You work cooperatively with others, being part of a team, and working together as opposed to working separately or competitively. You enjoy share responsibility and rewards for accomplishments. You actively participate and enjoy building the capability of the team. You maintain cooperative working relationships. You build team identity and spirit. You promote a friendly, cooperative climate in groups or organizations.

Also, we need an understanding of how we can have an effect on other people is vital. The more skills you have, the more respected you are for your abilities, the more people will listen to you. Content skills, such as expertise or reputation building and becoming the subject matter expert person for a particular topic are important. Process skills including researching, planning and facilitation are fundamental to constructing a well-timed and systematic approach. Right now, you are at an important step in building self awareness and relationships with others. You are learning to accept feelings, both good and bad. You understand that denial of your feelings can damage future relationships from pent-up emotions that can erupt as negative behavior, anger or that cause you to shut down emotionally.

Personality Drives Relationship Success

As leaders, we need to understand that our personalities have always played a key role in our relationships. They play an emotionally compelling role. We now know the secret is how we transmit our emotions. That is why emotional intelligence abilities are so crucial, the greater skill, the more forcefully emotions will increase performance for getting work done. Group and individual emotional intelligence requires the same capabilities: self-awareness, self-management, social awareness, and relationship management. Emotional intelligence relates to both individuals and the group as a whole at the same time. As a leader, we have responsibilities setting the ground rules for the team. The leader is the one who has the power to establish norms, and is responsible for maximizing harmony and collaboration to ensure that the team benefits from the best talents of each member. When core values and norms are clear to people, a leader does not even need to be physically present for the organization to run successfully. Emotional intelligence contributes to effective leadership by focusing on five essential elements of leader effectiveness: development of collective goals and objectives; instilling in others an appreciation of the importance of work activities; generating and maintaining enthusiasm, confidence, optimism, cooperation, and trust; encouraging flexibility in decision making and change; and establishing and maintaining a meaningful identity for an organization. An important dimension of leadership practice is patience and the ability to tolerate frustration and anxiety. This capability can help you as a leader to retain the capacity to think in the present moment, even in the face of uncertainty.

Emotional intelligence enables you to tune into other people, to empathize with them, to communicate clearly with them, to inspire and motivate them, to understand the relationship between you both. With emotional intelligence, you can inspire other people, develop their trust in you very quickly, and create a team that performs rather than storms, get innovative projects completed to deadlines. Emotional intelligence helps us both know and manage ourselves well, and the intelligence we have that helps us understand, motivate and relate effectively to other people.

Every day there are transactions between people. I am particularly interested in transactions that are positive, affectionate expressions of recognition which constitute the development of effective relationships and bonding experiences. The undeniable evidence is that anger, anxiety and depression, on one hand, and genuine relationship on the other, affect health and recovery from illness.

Businesses, organizations and people are changing. People are seeking their meaning and purpose in life. People are trying to find their passion. Along with our experiences, our brain also records the associated feelings, and both feelings and experiences stay locked together. It is possible for a person to exist in two states simultaneously because people can replay hidden experiences and feelings and are able to talk objectively about them at the same time. People have hidden experiences which are replayed in living color, and affect how they feel at the time of replaying.

We have heard the term of the "games" that people play. Games that people play start at an early age and we build our lives around our favorite games. Unfortunately, these games that people play may be fun in the beginning, but as time passes and with their repetitive toxic outcomes, games promote dysfunctional, life-long scripts. Transactional analysis is a communication skill in relationships and at work. Transactional methods are used to help us obtain much needed recognition by identifying our ego states and evaluating and improving the ways in which our ego states function, to recognize the inner dialogues between our ego states, especially those that involve a harsh demeaning Parent, to recognize the games that people play and to help us stop playing games and get recognition in a spontaneous aware and intimate and manner. Likewise as consultants, educators, counselors and life coaches with skills in analyzing transactional patterns are able to understand predict and help improve dysfunctional, unproductive, toxic, uncooperative interactions between people. We can quickly help people communicate clearly and effectively at the three levels of the Parent (values,) the Adult (rationality) and the Child (emotions, creativity).

When we communicate, we are doing so from one of our own three alter ego states: Our Parent (Parent is our 'Taught' concept of life), Adult (Adult is our 'Thought' concept of life) or Child (Child is our 'Felt' concept of life). If a crossed transaction occurs, ineffective communication follows. Attention is focused on the relationship. There are clues as to the ego state sending the signal. For example, in the Parent mode, we see (physical), anger or impatient body-language and expressions, finger-pointing, and patronizing gestures. In verbal, we hear words such as always, never, for once and for all, judgmental words, critical words, patronizing language, and posturing language. In the Adult mode, we see (physical), attentive, interested, straight-forward, tilted head, non-threatening and non-threatened. It is estimated that only seven percent of meaning is in the words spoken. There is no general rule as to the effectiveness of any ego state in any given situation (some people get results by being dictatorial (Parent to Child), or by having temper tantrums, (Child to Parent), but for a balanced approach to life, Adult to Adult is generally recommended. Transactional Analysis is effectively a language within a language; a language of true meaning, feeling and motive.

Transactional Analysis includes a theory of personality, a model of communication and a study of repetitive patterns of behavior. Previously Transactional Analysis suggested that effective communication was complementary (response echoing the path of the stimulus), and better still complementary adult to adult. Today, it is suggested that effective communications and relationships are based on complementary transactions to and from positive quadrants, and also, still, adult to adult. Stimuli and responses can come from any ego state, to any of the respondent's ego states. Understanding transactional analysis will enrich your dealings with people, and your understanding of yourself.

A Mind Thing, Female and Male Approach to Thinking

Experience tells us that not everything about how men and women approach thinking and relationship is biology or brain circuits. There is a link between cognition and the underlying brain structures. A lot has to do with the nurturing we received in our life. However, all of our experiences are impinging on our brain and adjusting the brain circuits that we are have at birth to be sex specific. There is no unisex brain. Gender identity is the subjective sense of being male or female. Our brains are what drive male or female impulses, values and our reality. I believe that men and women brains are different, some of the differences are innate and some induced by the social environment. The innate include neurological differences between men and women, women perceiving the world differently from men. There are inherent differences between male and female brains and which explains why women approach thinking and relationships naturally different from men. Research indicates that the sex hormone testosterone moulds the developing male brain, the areas responsible for communication, emotion and memory. Brain circuits for communication and emotional memory, in females develop unabated by high testosterone level of males. Men make 10 to 100 times more testosterone. As a result, females have more brains circuits for communications and reading emotions; able to use both sides of the brain. Female verbal and emotional circuits are enhanced with increased sensitivity and growth of emotion. Females develop earlier maturation of decision making and emotional control circuits, major interests in finding a mate, love, career development and emotional bonding. In males, that area of the brain are pared back, this result in boys and men speaking less than females and struggling to express their emotions to the same extent. Men listen with only one side of their brains, while women use both. This also affects the way men hear or don't hear other points of views. Many of the differences between the male and female personality can be explained by culture. Other differences such as verbal fluency, spatial reasoning are evident across cultures and may have both biological and learned determinants by social conditioning, with our upbringing greatly influencing our character.

Normal for men may be different than normal for women. Men, because we tend to compartmentalize our communication into a smaller part of the brain, tend to be better at getting t to the bottom of an issue. The female brain gathers a lot of material, gathers a lot of information, feels a lot, hears a lot, and senses a lot. There are hereditary or genetic differences between men and women. Women are born with two X chromosomes, and men with an X and a Y. There are at least 21 distinctive genes on the Y chromosome that are uniquely male. These genes control many of the male body's operations down to the level of the cells. Unfortunately, it doesn't explain why some men leave the toilet seat up, or some women can't take out the garbage. Men and women think differently but not that differently.

Scientists say males have more activity in mechanical centers of the brain, whereas females show more activity in verbal and emotional centers. Men and women's brains are distinctly different. Men have more neurons in the cerebral cortex. Women on the other hand have four times as many brain cells (neurons) connecting the right and left side of their brain. Women can focus on more than one problem at one time and frequently prefer to solve problems through multiple activities at a time. Males possess more tightly packed and more numerous nerve cells (neurons) than females. Females tend to have more neuropil, the fibular tissue that fills the space between nerve cell bodies and contains mainly nerve cell processes (synapses, dendrites and axons) that enable neurons to communicate with numerous other nerve cells. The recognition of gender-specific ways of thinking and feeling is more credible given these established differences could prove beneficial in enhancing interpersonal relationships.

Men and women approach problems with similar goals but with different considerations. While men and women can solve problems equally well, their approach and their process are often quite different. Women are usually more concerned about how problems are solved than merely solving the problem itself. The process of solving a problem can strengthen or weaken a relationship. Men approach problems in a very different manner than women. For most men, solving a problem presents an opportunity to demonstrate their competence, their strength of resolve, and their commitment to a relationship. Men have a tendency to dominate and to assume authority in a problem solving process. Men do not focus well on the quality of the relationship while solving problems.

Researchers report that functional magnetic resonance images (fMRI) show the brains of men and women respond differently to stimulation. Neuro-scientific research suggests how the brain develops and manifests personality and behavior. Both men and women express joy and pain and other emotions, however, they process and express them differently. Men have a greater link between the left brain, logic, and women have a greater connection to the right brain, the seat of emotions. In numerous studies in various cultures, boys and men have been found to be consistently less accurate at interpreting unspoken messages in gestures, facial expressions and tone of voice. Men also react less intensely to emotions-and forget them faster. Men use fewer words, and they talk, at least in public, as a means of putting themselves in a one up situation-unlike women, who talk to draw others closer.

Many researchers say, even at rest and without stimuli; a key part of men's and women's brains behaves differently. In men, the right amygdale, the structures in the center of the brain that are principally responsible for motor tasks that is involved with aspects of emotion and memory formation is more active and shows more connections with other regions of the brain. Conversely, in women, the left amygdala is more connected with other regions of the brain. In addition, the regions of the brain with which the amygdala communicates while a subject is at rest are different in men and women. As a researcher, it is intriguing because they provide the first hint of what could be a fundamental difference in how the brain is wired in men and women. If, even in a resting state, the brain shows such differences between the sexes, it could have far-reaching implications for medical and healthcare initiative.

Imagine that there is a difference between men and women as to which hemisphere's amygdala was more active, and also that the regions of the brain that the amygdala "talked" with were also quite different. Specifically, in men, the right-hemisphere amygdale, the part of the brain, associated with feelings of fear and aggression and important for visual learning and memory shows more connectivity with brain regions such as the visual cortex and the striatum. Conversely, many regions connected to the left-hemisphere amygdala in women control aspects of the environment within the body. For example, women have had to deal with a number of internal stressors, such as childbirth, that men haven't experienced. Men and women use different sides of their brains to process and store long-term memories.

Males possess more tightly packed nerve cells (neurons) than females. This may explain previous findings that women are more prone to certain illnesses than are men. Although a man and woman may lose the same number of neurons due to a disease, such as dementia, the woman's functional loss may be greater because the cells lost are more densely connected with other neurons. The recognition of gender-specific ways of thinking and feeling may be more credible given these established differences and could prove beneficial in enhancing interpersonal relationships.

We need to understand the differences between men and women. For centuries, the differences were socially defined and distorted through a lens of sexism in which men assumed superiority over women and maintained it through domination. As equality between men and women grows closer we are also losing our awareness of important differences. In some circles of society, politically correct thinking is obliterating this important discussion, as well as our awareness of the similarities and differences between men and women. The vision of equality between the sexes has narrowed the possibilities for discovery of what truly exists within a man and within a woman.

It is my position that men and women are equal but different. Men and women are physically different. The physical differences between men and women may provide functional advantages. Men are essentially built for physical confrontation and the use of force. A man's skull is almost always thicker and stronger than a woman's. The stereotype that men are more "thick-headed" than women is not far-fetched. A man's "thick headedness" and other anatomical differences have been associated with a uniquely male attraction to high-speed activities and reckless behavior that usually involve collisions with other males or automobiles. Contrary to women for example, men often fight with their fists rather than with words. Men invented the game "chicken."

Relationships between men and women are not impossible, or necessarily difficult. After all, not all men and women live in completely different realities. The challenge facing men and women is to become aware of their identities, to accept their differences, and to live their lives fully and as skillfully as possible. The following illustrates some important differences between men and women. These differences are not absolute. They describe how men and women are in most situations most of the time.

Men and women approach problems with similar goals equally well but with different considerations. While men and women can solve problems equally well, their approach and their process are often quite different. For most women, sharing and discussing a problem presents an opportunity to explore, deepen or strengthen the relationship with the person they are talking with. Women are usually more concerned about how problems are solved than merely solving the problem itself. The process of solving a problem can strengthen or weaken a relationship. Most men are less concerned about feelings when solving a problem. For most men, solving a problem presents an opportunity to demonstrate their competence, their strength of resolve, and their commitment to a relationship. Men have a tendency to dominate and to assume authority in a problem-solving process. Between males, relationships tend to be co-equal. Females tend to work their way through the maze as a group.

In general, men and women consider and process information differently. Women tend to be intuitive global thinkers. Women come to understand and consider problems all at once. Men come to understand and consider problems one piece at a time. Women have an enhanced ability to recall memories that have strong emotional components. Men tend to recall events using strategies that rely on reconstructing the experience in terms of elements, tasks or activities that took place. Profound experiences that are associated with competition or physical activities are more easily recalled. There appears to be a structural and chemical basis for observed memory differences. For instance, the hypocampus, the area in the brain primarily responsible for memory, reacts differently to testosterone in men and it reacts differently to changing levels of estrogen and progesterone in women. Women tend to remember or be reminded of different "emotional memories."

There is evidence to suggest that a great deal of the sensitivity that exists within men and women has a physiological basis. In both men and women, higher levels of testosterone directly affect the aggressive response and behavior centers of the brain. Increasing the estrogen and progesterone level in men has a "feminizing" effect. For men, what demonstrates a solid relationship is quite different from that of most women. Men feel closer and validated through shared activities. Such activities include sports, competition, outdoor activities or sexual activities that are decidedly active and physical. For example, women tend to equate sex with intimacy more so than men. While both men and women can appreciate and engage in these activities they often have preferential differences. Women, on the other hand, feel closer and validated through communication, dialogue and intimate sharing of experience, emotional content and personal perspectives. Many men tend to find such sharing and involvement uncomfortable, if not, overwhelming.

Today, there are challenges facing men and women which requires learning to accept their differences. This also includes avoiding the trap of taking their differences as personal attempts to frustrate each other, and to compromising whenever possible. Counseling and therapy can help a couple understand and appreciate each other, and even benefit from their differences. Understanding these differences intellectually is not enough. The differences that can be sensed between a man and women can deepen their relationship.

Personality Helps in Making Decisions

All or our interactions have an emotional aspect that we may ignore. Focusing on our emotional side as well as our intelligence side means we try to include our emotions for effective, productive problem-solving and relationship-building. We also look at the organized, structured way we analyze problems. To put it another way, you need to understand how sensitive you are to your own feelings and the feelings of others, so that you can better understand your behavior and make better decisions. We involve our entire personality in making decisions, not just the formal, well thought-out analysis of the problem. In making any decision, you should understand how your decision makes you feel in terms of: do you feel right, what is your gut or physical, did you "open up" in the right way, can you effectively persuade others to accept your ideas without coercing them, do you hold onto problems, anger, or hurts from the past and cannot move beyond these.

Ideally, it would be a good thing for you to have a greater understanding of your personality and behavior styles. Prepared with knowledge about your current styles, you can make more informed choices about the kinds of behaviors you want to demonstrate in the future and increase your success and satisfaction in your career and interpersonal interactions. In different situations, do you fake being nice, or tough, or calm and collected because you think those are appropriate characteristics? Are you a human doormat? Do you say "yes" when you mean "no"? Assertiveness is the ability to formulate and communicate one's own thoughts, opinions and wishes in a clear, direct, and non-aggressive way. Do you keep your opinions to yourself for fear of upsetting or confronting others? A lack of assertiveness or weak communication skills may be keeping you from fulfilling your potential and reaching your goals. Are you oriented towards the outer world or the inner world? Are you most comfortable in throngs of people, or do you prefer your own company? Would you classify yourself as shy or outgoing? Whether you fall in the extrovert or introvert category or somewhere in between has a large influence on your career choice, relationships and overall lifestyle. Do you often find yourself unable to control your temper? Does your anger come out in unhealthy ways that are damaging to both yourself and others? Anger is an extremely powerful emotion, and an inability to keep it under control can lead to serious problems in relationships, career and families. How long can you focus on a task before you start "zoning out"? How do you know if you're a perfectionist? Are you putting unreasonable demands on yourself by setting the bar too high? Do you expect too much from your family or loved one? Or feel that the world is exerting pressure on you? You might be a perfectionist. Do you believe in yourself? Do you give yourself the credit you deserve? Self-esteem is an integral part of personal happiness, fulfilling relationships and achievement. Your values are a set of attitudes, unique to you, which govern your behavior and guide the way you look at the world. Each individual seeks to achieve certain goals in life, and his or her values are in tune with these goals. For instance, some individuals may see their family life as most important to them. They hold values that illustrate this- they believe that spending time with their family is more important then working long hours, and they may disagree with individuals whom they perceive as holding a more work-oriented value system. Looking back at their life, they hope to see that their family was always their top priority. Clarifying our values now can help us prioritize our lives in order to avoid disappointment and unhappiness later in life. Living a life in tune with our values is important because they are what determine what means most to us. Do you control your destiny or are you controlled by it? A locus of control orientation is a belief about whether the outcomes of our actions are contingent on what we do (internal control orientation) or on events outside our personal control (external control orientation). Our attribution style determines which forces we hold responsible for our successes and failures. Both locus of control and attribution styles have great influence on our motivation, expectations, self-esteem, risk-taking behavior, and even on the actual outcome of our actions. What is your locus of control? And what forces are responsible for your successes and failures?

    Imagine hearing someone describe you and you wondered who they were talking about. Research suggests we don't know ourselves as well as we think we do. Our identities may change based on our surroundings including social feedback, comparison with others, society's perception of our behavior challenge us to redefine ourselves. Individual levels of self-awareness vary. Those struggling to define themselves seek feedback to help enhance their self-awareness, he says, whereas those with a strong identity rely less on feedback: People reinterpret, reject or accept information based on their own understanding of self.

    Getting feedback is necessary in all relationships. You need to share your feelings about the way you interact, like it or not. But getting and receiving feedback is hard. In fact, giving and getting feedback can be stressful depending on how you view the feedback e.g., friendly and not hurtful. Feedback can be interpreted in many different ways depending on how you view the person giving it, friend or enemy. To receive feedback efficiently, you must learn how to listen. Sharpening your listening skills can de-escalate potential conflict and avoid misunderstandings. By hearing what the other person has to say, you stand a better chance of understanding the issue. This considerate approach opens the way to an exchange of views; it will also help the giver and the receiver agree on a plan of action on conflict.

In taking a personal accounting of your personality, you need to take a step back especially when there is an issue. You need to understand and work on yourself first and how do you see the problem. Once this happens, you will find that there will be much less finger pointing and much more cooperation. Your emotional intelligence is a part of your behavioral personality, and personality provides the perspective in which emotional intelligence operates. Personality can be defined as your pattern of internal experience and social interaction that arises from your action, your major psychological subsystems. Your major psychological subsystems involve emotion, cognition, and the self, among others.

Keep these suggestions in mind:

- Ask open-ended questions. Questions that begin with the words "tell me" or "how."

- Avoid being emotional. Allow yourself to remain calm and thoughtful. Think before you respond.

- Summarize what the person you are talking to is saying for feedback clarification and understand.

- Ask to receive your feedback in private.

- Seek regular feedback. If feedback is given often, communication will be continuous.

- Avoid being aggressive, sarcastic or confrontational feedback and responses to the feedback giver.

Point out the areas where you agree with the other person.

- Don't be rigid and attached to your point of view. Be open-minded to different outcomes.

- Don't fall into the "defend and attack" trap.

Who are you is a good question. What differentiates you from another person and why you behave the way that you do. As you know when we generalize, it doesn't apply to all people. To illustrate, consider the generalization that men are generally taller than women. This does not mean that every man is taller than every woman. Instead, it means that, on average, men are taller than women. This same generalization applies to the feedback that is given on a personality questionnaire or survey. Even though, on average, people tend to become more conscientious as they get older, not everyone follows this pattern.

Many people ask, "Why is the personality profile feedback sometimes different from how I see myself?" Feedback is not meant to suggest that everyone who scores high on Extraversion or some other trait will be exactly as we describe them. Feedback is based on generalizations derived from research. It is unavoidable that some people will not fit every generalization. Also, people asked, "Why do personality feedback sometimes give contradictory information?" Again, this is a result of making generalizations. Individuals cannot be captured by the general trends derived from analysis of large numbers of people. Generalizations are not always correct but overall, they are useful.

People living in different regions of the country have different personalities. It could be that people high in openness move to places that are densely populated and culturally diverse. Alternatively, living in densely populated and culturally diverse place may cause people to become more open. For that reason, birthplace, place of residence, and how long you have lived in each region have implications for the link between your personality and environment.

There are a number of personality types and traits that may or may not apply to you. For illustration, please select a number next to each statement to indicate the extent to which you agree or disagree with that statement. Each trait is clarified by a number of characteristics, so you should rate the extent to which the set as a whole applies to you generally, even if some characteristics apply more strongly than others: (Strongly Disagree; Disagree somewhat; Disagree a little; Neither disagree or agree; Agree a little; Agree somewhat; Strongly Agree)

I see myself as:

- Extraverted, enthusiastic
- Critical, quarrelsome
- Dependable, self-disciplined
- Anxious, easily upset
- Open to new experiences, complex

- Reserved, quiet
- Sympathetic, warm
- Disorganized, careless
- Calm, emotionally stable

The Enneagram personality test maps nine distinct personalities and the extremes within each type that can be seen when a person is under stress or thriving. The word is from the Greek - ennea, meaning nine, and gram, meaning points or types. It is represented by a circle with nine numbered points around the circumference. Each person is dominant with one type of personality, we are also influenced by the traits of the personality types on either side, or the "wings," The Enneagram of personality type, is a business tool that I believe, helps us to understand ourselves and others, focusing our awareness through the prism of the Enneagram. Enneatype descriptions can range from extremely healthy (noble or altruistic) to extremely unhealthy (psychotic). It helps us understand our whole personality, from our greatest desires and concerns all the way to our most mundane behaviors and reactions. For Enneagram personality type illustration, the following may be observed:

- A perfectionist is driven to do the "right" thing and prone to repressed anger.
- A helper needs to be needed. An achiever is efficient, goal-driven and focused on being a "winner" concerned with appearances-style over substance, can crowd out friends, family and self-awareness.
- An individualist craves self-expression and emotional depth.
- An observer is perceptive and capable of synthesizing information in new ways, protective of privacy, personal resources and prone to emotional detachment.
- A team-player is vigilant for threats from the environment, loyal and engaging, but full of contradictions which create self-doubt and indecisiveness.
- A leader is driven to control self and environment, capable of both domination and protectiveness.

It may surprise you that personality may be the reason why your spouse/significant other/love ones/boss drives you up the wall, or why they can't seem to get along with a particular colleague, their mother-in-law, or friend. If you want to know what type of job or relationship would suit you best, a personality analysis such as Myers-Briggs Type Indicator (MBTI) based on Jungian psychology can help. If you want something that is going to tell you what sort of partner you may get on with, what kind of job would suit you, or even how inclined you are towards growth, MBTI is a useful tool. Myers-Briggs is used in workplaces for conflict management and team building, for career counseling, for relationship conflicts, and just by people who want a better idea of who they are and what challenges they face. MBTI is useful for all types of relationships because it's about how you communicate, what needs you have, and what issues you need to deal with. It's also about understanding differences, which is not only desirable but a necessity, especially with today diversity.

The Myers-Briggs is an assessment, not a test. You can't pass or fail. And it has nothing to do with skills or abilities. Rather, it presents you with a series of questions designed to find out your natural personality type, specifically, whether you lean towards "extroversion" or "introversion"; "sensing" or "intuition"; "thinking" or "feeling"; and "perception" or "judging" not to be confused with judgmental. You can develop all these preferences, but some are easier, or more attractive to you, than others. Having a general understanding of how the different types work can also give you a greater insight into yourself, as well as other people.

The Myers-Briggs model of personality is based on four preferences, although there are 16 combinations of these. The first preference deals with where you prefer to direct your energy. If it's towards people, things, situations, or "the outer world", then your preference is for Extroversion (E). If it's towards dealing with ideas, information, explanations or beliefs, or "the inner world", then your preference is for Introversion (I). We all deal with both worlds. The Es feel deprived when cut-off from interaction with the outside world, while the Is need private time to recharge their batteries. The second preference relates to how you process information. If you prefer to deal with facts, your preference is for Sensing (S). If you prefer to deal with ideas, or what isn't obvious, then your preference is Intuition (N). Some people are factual (S) and others gather information through intuition or gut feeling (N)," explains McGuiness. S types dislike guessing when facts are "fuzzy"; Ns use their imagination to create new explanations or possibilities. The third preference looks at how you process information or make decisions. If you prefer to decide on the basis of objective logic, using an analytical and detached approach, your preference is for Thinking (T). Those who like to decide something based on values and/or personal beliefs are Feeling (F). The Myers-Briggs Type Indicator looks at how you prefer to organize your life. If you prefer your life to be planned, stable and organized then your preference is for Judging

(J). If you prefer to go with the flow, to maintain flexibility and respond to things as they arise, then your preference is for Perception (P). When you put these four letters together, you get your Myers-Briggs type code. In making a decision there is always a struggle between making the decision and waiting for more information.

Tap into Your Dormant Power, Fear

Many of us are passive, held back by fear. Whether we like it or not, our thoughts affect how we experience life. Negative thinking makes us passive and positive thinking has been credited with the success of most successful people. Additionally, positive thinking impacts our health, well-being, and motivation. Fear can have a crippling effect in our personal life and for that reason alone, we need to conquer fear. Conquering fear is not simple, it requires courage. Fear is based on the uncertainty of change and the lack of positive self-image.

Choices are not opportunities to make mistakes, but valid paths to growth, whichever path we take. Fear is caused by the belief that we can't handle whatever we're called upon to face. We may also be crippled by insecurity. We believe that our future is full of dangers. Fear is a handicap with which we must learn to cope.

We begin by unlearning the misconceptions about fear and replacing them with attitudes of strength and conviction. By mixing positive thinking with situational experiences that reflect our basic fear responses, we begin to understand that fear is what we make of it, and that in most cases unfounded. When we are fearful, faulty thinking is most often the real culprit; when we corrected this type of thinking, our fear is gone. While there is no quick fix, we should be encouraged and begin where we are. Start using positive-thinking as a tool to overcome a variety of common fears. We have tremendous untapped dormant powers within us, which can be harnessed for success with the proper attitude. Be inspired by this important message. I hope this book will serve as a helpful reminder as you continue on your journey of success and fulfillment.

Promise yourself that you will dare to dream and follow your passion, then watch your vision unfold before you as you make it happen! Promise yourself to be strong when faced with hard times so that nothing disturbs your peace of mind. Share positive thought and words of health, happiness and prosperity to every person you meet. Reconnect with special friends and make them feel they are of value to you. The bigger the promise, the more you must look at the sunny side of everything and make your optimism come true. Think only of the best, to work only for the best and to expect only the best, you deserve nothing less than the best. Be as enthusiastic about the success of others as you are about your own. Forgive yourself, forget the mistakes of the past, and press on to the greater achievements of the future. Be happy and cheerful at all times and share your special smile with everyone you meet. Focus on your promise to yourself, and self improvement. Do not waste time listening to or criticizing others. Be positive and try not to worry, anger and fear will destroy you from within. We can turn our passivity into assertiveness by taking time to take action to stop negative thinking patterns and reeducate our mind to think more positively. We need to not let our fear stop us…fear not, abundant life is yours…carpe diem…just go for it! Promise yourself to be yourself, be your best self and make a difference in yourself and the world.

Reaching Your Potential and the 80/20 Rule

In the 19th century, Vilfredo Pareto, an Italian economist, conducted a study on income and wealth patterns. He discovered a "predictable imbalance" that shows up in every area of life. This is now known as the Pareto Time Principle, or the 80/20 Rule. We need to understand the 80/20 Rule, known as the Principle, or the 80/20 Rule. In 1906, it was observed that 80% of the land in Italy was owned by 20% of the population. Later, researchers discovered that this principle was valid in other parts of life. The 80/20 Rule means that 80% of time spent poorly produces 20% of desired results, while 20% of time spent wisely nets 80% of the desired results. Although the "80/20" Rule is only arbitrary, it can be used to achieve extraordinary results from your time. For example, for time management it means that twenty percent of the things on your "To Do" list will bring you eighty percent of the value you need to be successful in your job. As a result, you will work hard at identifying that important twenty percent. The best place to start managing time better is with yourself by managing your time and not let time manage you. When you face the fact that you may be the cause of some of your time problems, you are ready to change your habits. You can get more done and be more productive in less time and with less effort.

Success is available to everyone. There is enough information contained in all the self-help books that could make us more financially secure, successful, and happy beyond our wildest dreams. So why aren't we more financially secure, successful, and happy? We aren't for a number of reasons. We are really quite happy to waste time watching TV or on other entertainment. With only three percent of the population being millionaires and billionaires, many people believe that, no matter how many books on personal development we read…success will pass some of us by. I believed that I suffered from the same problem…until circumstances changed my life…that's when I literally stumbled upon the keys to reaching my fullest potential, success. Success requires hard work…but it requires the right sort of hard work. The hard work that I am referring to requires getting along with other people and people skills is critical. It requires developing our skills a little every day. With a positive outlook, there are no limits to what you can achieve and there is no reason to stop yourself from reaching your dreams. The only difference between an ordinary person and an extra ordinary person, or the only difference between you and a successful person is doing something a little extra to become extraordinary and successful.

In any situation, there are usually a few people or factors whose influence far surpasses the importance of other people or other factors. The 80/20 Principle is present is many aspect of our lives, both personally, and professionally. On our jobs or in our business, according to the rule or principle, 80% of the work or a company's profits are generated by twenty percent of the workers or its customers. By identifying and ranking the workforce or customers in order of efficiency or profitability, you can then focus your workload or sales efforts on these vital few employees or customers. In advertising, approximately eighty percent of the results of an ad campaign will be produced by twenty percent of the advertising. By focusing on the effectiveness of ads, a great deal of advertising could be eliminated, and those funds committed to the advertising that is producing the desired results.

The 80/20 Rule can be applied to our personal life, as well. Take personal productivity for example, eighty percent of our time is currently spent on trivial activities. In our personal life, twenty percent of our activities are producing eighty percent of our results. We need to begin to focus only on the twenty percent activities that will help us to reach our full potential (happiness), and either discontinue or delegate the eighty percent time waster activities. Whatever your answer, try to strive to increase the frequency of your twenty percent activity and to some extent people that encourage you, that is producing the results you desired results. In relationships, we need to ask, what activities create the most desired results in our relationships? Once we identify these activities, we need to shift our focus so that we are concentrating on these vital few activities. In health, eighty percent of our health is produced by twenty percent of the foods we're eating. By acting on our observations, we will enhance our potential and the results we produce both at work, and in our personal life.

Principles

- Likability is important in all relationships and serves to complement the person you are, not replace who you are.

- Your purpose is a reflection of the likeable you.

DREAM GREATNESS BE UNSTOPPABLE

5
SELF-TRUST, AWARENESS AND FEARLESSNESS

"We have come over a way that with tears has been watered, we have come, reading our path through the blood of the slaughtered."

— James Weldon Johnson, *Lift Every Voice and Sing*

Trust in Yourself

The more we learn to trust our own values and accept others, even when we don't agree, the more peace and freedom we will have in our own lives. When you develop the qualities of self-trust, awareness, and fearlessness, the natural consequence of these will be optimism. You'll have good reason to be optimistic because you'll have the assets of happiness, high levels of motivation, and passion driven by your desire to serve others working for you. Fear is a major barrier in developing trust and in realizing your dreams. Trust in yourself and you'll be able to handle challenges that would have previously paralyzed you because fear will no longer be part of your thinking.

There are aspects of trust we must embody in our daily actions that translate simply to being fair, open, honest and caring. Trust is found in the heart. People will follow those they trust. For people to trust you, you must work on:

- Knowing yourself, being yourself, allowing yourself to be known.
- Speaking your truth and speaking it consistently.
- Connecting well with others.

- Erring on the side of over-communicating.
- Listening to people and inspiring and guiding them with constant empathy.
- Being humble and giving credit for accomplishment.
- Being willing to openly and sincerely apologize as soon as you realize you've erred.
- Being willing to ask for help, recognizing you can't do it all yourself.
- Being willing to consistently go the final yard to get the job done.
- Possessing a strong intuitive capacity for making tough decisions with appropriate input in a timely manner.
- Focusing on your passion for living your heart and vision.
- Hiring great people, coaching them and delegating responsibilities equal to their maturity and skills.
- Being firm and demanding but never mean-spirited.
- Having conviction but also being flexible and adaptable.
- Staying the course in the face of temporary set-backs.
- Developing and maintaining constancy of purpose.
- Having a passion and sharing that passion and create an environment of collaboration.
- Developing and maintaining congruency to really caring about people and not being a hypocrite.
- Being open to participation, trying new ideas and innovation.

Trust-centered relationship applies to any setting and any endeavor, from how you lead your family, your organizations and yourself. It reminds us that we must constantly work to be worthy of our supporter, for without them, we are alone. Trust and success is complex and continuous. Your emotional style sets the tone for building trust. But cultivating trust can make it easier, to develop an understanding of the impact of your words and actions, and learn how to navigate interactions and disarm conflict, identifying ways to improve collaboration across stakeholders. Trust building focuses on the core components of emotional intelligence that leaders need to be successful: self-awareness; self-management; social awareness; and relationship management, especially these confusing times.

In "*The 7 Habits of Highly Effective People*," Stephen R. Covey suggests a simple metaphor, an Emotional Bank Account to describe "the amount of trust that's been built up in a relationship." The emotional banks account is "the amount of trust that's been built up in a relationship." Trust is needed for a relationship to thrive. As with any bank account, actions (trust worthy) or deposits accumulates positive balances by deposits and other actions (breaches in trust) produces negative balances by withdrawals. It is a simple, yet effective metaphor for how we establish and sustain trust or erode and diminish trust in our personal and professional relationships. Without trust, we may manage to put up and with a person for a while but not in the long run. Trust has been identified as a key element of successful conflict resolution including negotiation and mediation. Trust is associated with enhanced cooperation, information sharing, and problem solving. The need for trust comes from our interdependence with other people. We often depend on other people to help us achieve, obtain or find something, or at least not to discourage or frustrate, the outcomes we value. As our interests with others are intertwined, we also must recognize that there is an element of risk involved insofar as we often encounter situations in which we cannot compel the cooperation we seek. Therefore, trust can be very valuable in social interactions.

Trust takes time to build and seconds to destroy. The consequences of abused trust can hurt a business, family, association or friendship. Trust is answerable and accountable. Trustworthiness is a crucial part of emotional maturity. If people do not trust you, you may have to give reason for and justify every detail of every decision. Trust is the result of good communication and constant maintenance. Relationships are based upon trust and cannot exist without it. We need to practice trust building from time to time. Trust may be defined as the antidote to the fears and risks attendant to meaningful commitment. Trust means confidence in others. When trust prevails, people more willing to go through difficulty and feel, supported through ups, downs, risk and potential loss. The experience of trust has been extensively explored by a variety of disciplines across the social sciences, including economics, social psychology, and political science. Trust is a mental state involving the intention to accept vulnerability based upon positive expectations of the intentions or behavior of another. Trust begins with your thoughts and continues with the willingness to act based on the words, actions, and decisions of another.

The need for trust arises from our interdependence with others. Theory on the origins of interpersonal trust has proceeded broadly along three fronts: explaining differences in the individual propensity to trust; understanding dimensions of trustworthy behavior; and suggesting levels of trust development. We all have the propensity to trust. Personality theorists have developed one of the oldest theoretical perspectives on trust, and argued that some people are more likely to trust than others. Our trust in another individual can be grounded in our evaluation of his/her ability, integrity, and benevolence. The effect of benevolence will increase as the relationship between the parties grows closer.

We have levels of trust development. Trust builds along a continuum of hierarchical and sequential stages, such that as trust grows to 'higher' levels, it becomes stronger and more resilient and changes in character. At early stages of a relationship, trust is at a mathematical-based level. Individuals deciding to trust the other mentally contemplate the benefits of staying in the relationship with the trustee versus the benefits of 'cheating' on the relationship, and the costs of staying in the relationship versus the costs of breaking the relationship. Trust is extended to the others based on this cost-benefit calculation to the degree that continued trust will yield a net positive benefit.

Driven by the numbers, mathematical-based trust is largely a cognitively-driven (IQ) trust phenomenon, grounded in our judgments to predict with reliability. This allows trust to grow to a higher level and qualitatively different level. At this stage trust has been built to the point that the parties have internalized each other's desires and intentions. Trust at the higher level is enhanced by a strong emotional bond between the parties, based on a sense of shared goals and values. Trust violations occur when our confident in another person is disconfirmed. These violations result lower subsequent trust, and may reduce the extent to which we will cooperate with the other person again.

We proceed to consider how violations damage interpersonal trust. In some cases, a single trust violation may seriously damage or irreparably destroy trust. In other cases, one trust violation may not be that damaging when considered in isolation. Rather, a pattern of violations may be needed to create serious damage to the relationship. In other words, not all trust violations are created equally. So, to analyze the effect of trust violations on a relationship, we need a way to describe how much harm (cognitive and/or emotional) a given violation has created. For example, minor offenses may be met with simply a reduced level of trust. Serious offenses harm trust severely, often to the point of complete destruction. The loss of trust depends on a number of things: the magnitude of the offense, number of prior violations, and pattern of violations. As the proverbial "straw that broke the camel's back," it is the pattern of trust violations that provides evidence that the offender is not worthy of future trust. However, when there are few past violations, any given trust violation may be viewed as the exception rather than the rule. I believe that trust depends on specific dimension of trust that was violated.

Relationships can become rather resilient to trust violations as long as the violations do not challenge the underlying basis of the relationship.

Trust violations occur when the victim's confident positive expectations of the offender are disconfirmed. These violations result lower subsequent trust, and may reduce the extent to which victims of these violations cooperate with the offender. The emotional reaction is likely to be a mixture of anger, disappointment, and/or frustration at oneself for trusting and at the offender for exploiting that trust. However, when the basis of a relationship becomes called into question by a trust violation e.g., marital infidelity, it can devastate the entire relationship. Rebuilding trust is not an easy task. After trust has been damaged, there are two key considerations for the victim: 1) dealing with the stress the violation imposed on the relationship, and 2) determining if future violations will occur. After a trust violation and the cognitive and affective fallout that ensues, the first critical question is, is the victim willing to reconcile? If the victim believes that the violator will not make efforts at correcting the wrongs and minimizing future violations, the victim has no incentive to attempt reconciliation and restore trust. Reconciliation occurs when both parties exert effort to rebuild a damaged relationship, and strive to settle the issues that led to the disruption of that relationship. In all relationships, actions may speak louder than words, so it is imperative for the offender to honor trust in subsequent interactions with tangible offerings designed to restore fairness in the relationship.

Both communication and action are essential to the trust rebuilding process, but relationship trust repair involves an emotional, relational focus. Trust building steps must be performed competently. Trust building entails a number of steps. When most people talk about trust, the emphasis usually is on the negative side of trust, or lack of trust. Trust enables relationships to develop and flourish. When trust erodes, the relationship deteriorates. When we trust, or don't trust someone, we are assessing their sincerity, reliability and competence. Trusting or not trusting someone always involves one or more of these assessments. The issue of trust is also linked with our identity. Trust can be regarded as a fragile element of relationships which needs continual nurturing.

Today, an increasing number of people are feeling trapped in an unfilled life. They are searching for something more, better health, greater wealth, more freedom, more meaning, fulfillment and happiness. Few people realize that they have the keys to unlocking their real potential and it is in the way they think. Our thoughts and feelings make and color our reality. Therefore, we must begin where we are and start thinking new positive thoughts and imagining how good we feel regardless of our current situation. As we think new thoughts, we begin realizing our dreams while helping others along the way. This is the universal law of life and how it works. Just by enhancing our thoughts and intuition, we can create the future we desire.

To achieve the dreams and ambitions which have eluded us most of our lives, we have to get off the sideline. We have to stop watching and admiring what other successful people are doing. Success is not a result of doing the right things or of being in the right place at the right time. Success comes from your thoughts and being the person in your dreams…being the right person. By now, we know that we attract to our lives not what we want but what we are. By thinking "excitement" you create an "exciting" life.

Our outer wealth is a reflection of our inner beliefs about self worth. And here's the best part! As we increase our self worth, we automatically attract better and better things into our life! Higher expectations mean higher results which is one of the universal laws of life. Universal laws are very simple. And once we consciously understand these laws, we will awaken our own wisdom and inner power. The universal order of life, the magnificence, the purpose and beauty of our own existence become clear. We have the inner power that will unlock our creativity and open up our true full potential. We have unlimited potential to achieve whatever we desire from life. We can learn how to attract love, happiness and abundance and once we learn this, we will experience increased inner peace and exhilaration.

It has been written that love is the discovery of ourselves in others and the delight in that recognition. Our inner journey takes us through the stages of love and fear. Love is in each of us. When we are born, we have unconscious love, we exist as pure love but we are not conscious of our love. Our wounds bring our conscious fear to love which causes pain and suffering that enable us to become conscious of our fears. Love is the remedy for suffering; a remedy for our pain. All roads lead to love. When we've suffered enough pain, we move onto conscious love, we are motivated to move through our fears to consciously experience love. Simply by discovering more inner peace, we experience the magic of knowing that we are, living our life the way we have chosen. Begin building inner trust and create your own world from the inside out. Be your true self and make a difference in your self and the world.

Trust is Necessary to Unlocking Dreams

Trust can be careful, measured, thoughtful, and conditional and still be authentic, not blind. But, trust requires a reciprocal relationship in which questions of probability take a back seat to questions of mutual expectations, responses, and commitments. Simple trust is unreflective. Blind trust is self-deceptive. Authentic trust is both reflective and honest with itself and others. All forms of trust involve counting on other people, and, as such, they all are vulnerable to betrayal. But whereas simple and blind trust experience betrayal as earth-shattering, betrayal or disappointment is neither surprising nor devastating to authentic trust. All trust involves vulnerability and risk, and nothing would count as trust if there were no possibility of betrayal or disappointment. But whereas simple trust is devoid of distrust, and blind trust denies the very possibility of distrust, authentic trust is articulated in such a way that it must recognize the possibilities for betrayal and disappointment. It has taken into account the arguments for distrust, but has nevertheless resolved itself on the side of trust. Authentic trust is thus complex, and it is anything but naive. Authentic trust is not opposed to distrust so much as it is in a continuing dialectic with it, trust and distrust defining each other in terms of the other.

Trust is seemingly in decline in contemporary society, yet its significance and value is undiminished. Numerous scandals afflicting business and politics, the growth of "spin" and a loss of faith in leaders have all eroded levels of trust. As trust becomes a scarcer commodity, those people and organizations that possess it have a distinct advantage. Trust makes us work together towards common goals. The social and moral aspects of trust were inherited from the ruling religious and political institutions since biblical times. The information revolution destroyed many of the well-established models of trust and created new others, most of them yet to be understood. Trust is the demonstrated belief in something or someone. When many people think of trust, it is usually about mistrust. Trust is fundamental to achieving success in life. If you cannot trust in anything, life becomes intolerable, a constant battle against paranoia and looming disaster. You can't have relationships without trust, let alone good ones. Intimacy depends on it. I suspect more marriages are wrecked by lack of trust than by actual infidelity. The partner who can't trust the other person not to betray him or her will either drive them away or force them into some real or assumed act of faithlessness.

Trust is essential in the workplace. An organization without trust will be full of backstabbing, fear and paranoid suspicion. If you work for a boss who doesn't trust their people to do things right, you'll have a miserable time of it. They'll be checking up on you all the time, correcting "mistakes" and "oversights" and constantly reminding you to do this or that. Colleagues who don't trust one another will need to spend more time watching their backs than doing any useful work. In this situation, people will resort to initiating pre-empted attacks to protect themselves. In the end, this will encourage more distrust and attacks ending only with the victory for the most brutal and cunning. If you have any idea you're working in a Machiavellian culture which includes assigning tasks that are destined to fail to an expendable member of staff so that they can be blamed for it going wrong, avoiding work or responsibility by pretending to be overstretched or overworked...if you ever feel like you're a victim, you've got to move on and go to a place where you feel comfortable.

Organizations are always trying to cut costs. Think of all the additional work caused directly by lack of trust. Audit departments only exist because of it. Companies keep voluminous records because they don't trust their suppliers, their contractors and their customers. Probably more than half of all administrative work is only there because of a pervasive sense that mistrust of anyone these days." If even a small part of such insignificant work could be removed, the savings would run into millions of dollars. If you took all that way, how much extra time would you suddenly find in your day? How much of your work pressure would disappear?

If you trusted other people more, you would not be so overworked, under constant pressure. Your trust would allow you to let others take on tasks and ease your burdens by delegating because you trust people to do what they've been asked to do. You will not have to attend every meeting, however futile, because you trust others not to talk about you behind your back, or to reach decisions you like. When you don't trust, you demand copies of every memo, report and e-mail, because you don't trust what might be said if you're not watching. You're constantly keyed-up and tense, watching for rivals or anyone perceive may try to launch some covert operation to undermine you position. Surprisingly, it is not the pressure of actual work that's driving people towards some stress-related illness, it is their lack of trust in anyone and anything. Is it any wonder that more and more people are close to total burnout?

Someone has to begin the cycle of trust by an act of faith. It's no use waiting for the other person to make the first move. In fact, people are waiting for you. It takes a conscious act of unconditional belief in that other person's good sense, ability, honesty or sense of commitment to set the ball rolling. Will your trust sometimes be misplaced? Of course, it will because life isn't perfect and some people aren't trustworthy. But will increasing your willingness to trust produces a positive benefit. Will it make your life more pleasant and less stressful? I believe so. With the pressure we are under, we have little to lose by trying. Trust has to start somewhere. Why not with you? Why not today? Why not right now?

Belief in a Just World

A part of having a dream is sharing it with others. It feels good give or to do something for someone else without being asked to do it. This is an unconditional gift of love. Look for opportunities to do good deeds for others or give them praise for their abilities. Goodwill can be contagious. We need to practice forgiveness. Forgiveness is more than just telling someone, "I forgive you", it comes from sincere intentions. This will free us from our negative feelings such as guilt, sadness, fear, anger and resentment. Knowledge is one thing, living what you learned is another. It takes time to change old ways of thinking but it is worth the time and effort. If we are willing to work at being consistent in what we think say and do, true happiness will be ours.

We are all partners on our journey and the greatest challenge in our road map to personal and professional success is to hold onto our values of sharing and caring that make us brothers and sisters on the road to our dreams. Social and emotional competence shapes your interaction with the people around you. Paying attention to the social, emotional and ethical development of ourselves can provide the framework for not only increasing your skill competency but help you tackle the deeper societal issues around prejudice, equity and justice. Many of us feel the intense pressure of living and working in uncertain times. You need of a deeper sense of community and more opportunities to develop a capacity for meaning and purpose in your life.

Most of us have been taught that we lived in a just world. A just world is a world where, ultimately, good people are rewarded and bad people are punished. Advertisers take advantage of our belief in a just world, when they display some desirable commodity and urge us to buy it because "You deserve it."

There are advantages to believing in a just world. When we see other people suffering we can protect ourselves from the pain of pity by telling ourselves that these people must have deserved what has happened to them. We can say, "If she hadn't been dressed like that she wouldn't have been raped" or "If he'd been positive in his outlook and looked after his health he wouldn't have developed cancer." As children we know only too well that if we are bad we get punished and if we are good we get rewarded, even if the only reward is that nothing bad happens to us.

Increasingly, you hear people say, "I've worked hard." Many people see their lack of success as a great disaster. How do we allocate blame? As much as we puzzle over this question, it allows only three possible answers: "It was my fault." "It was someone else's fault." or "It happened by chance." However, in the just world, nothing happens by chance. If we believe in the just world, when a disaster strikes we can ask only whether it was our fault or someone else's fault. Blaming ourselves for the disaster is what turns the sadness that appropriately follows loss into the prism of depression. If we see that we live in a world where things happen by chance, we are in a better position to work out what is actually going on. By believing in a just world, people prevent themselves from seeing that in law, as in every profession, advancement and success are very much a matter of chance. Certainly, if we work hard we are likely to improve our chances of doing well, but by no means does hard work lead to success. No amount of goodness prevents disaster.

Nowadays, many people include in their definition of goodness having a positive attitude. If we believe that goodness can prevent disasters, we believe that our thoughts, a positive attitude can influence events. We all know that this is magical thinking, and people who use it are failing to think logically. Certainly stress and depression can affect our health, but this is not a matter of the painful thoughts that make up stress and depression acting directly on the body. Positive attitudes and a lack of fear can help maintain the efficient functioning of the immune system, but a positive attitude (goodness) alone cannot protect us from all the ills that can befall us.

We create ideas that we treat as absolute truths and thus imprison ourselves. Society's rules that boys must not cry and that girls must not be competitive are not absolute laws of the universe, though many people treat them as if they are. They are simply ideas that people have constructed. For example, many people make themselves miserable by relating myths as facts about life, after forty life is downhill all the way. No wonder many people find it hard to accept turning forty. Another assumption concerns what we inherit from our parents. All a gene does is express a little protein. There are thousands of proteins interacting in extremely complex, constantly changing ways, very little of which is understood. As a result, even disorders that are genetic, such as cystic fibrosis, are not understood, as the very limited success of gene therapy shows. People will say, from a depressed mother, we will gain many dysphoric, fearful ideas, and an ill-tempered father will fail to teach us effective methods of dealing with anger. However, claiming that we have inherited our father's bad temper or our mother's propensity to become depressed has one great advantage: it relieved us of responsibility for the effect that our behavior has on other people. But our refusal to be held accountable to change our behavior diminished the affection people have had for us, and their unloving, unfriendly reactions to us add to our misery.

Our immediate interpretations of what happens to us derive from assumptions we have made about the world and about how we should live our lives. Many people learned about the just world in their religious education, at home, and at school. Ideas that have helped us at some point in our lives can become the source of our misery at another time. Belief in the just world has led many to becoming bitter and resentful. By seeing that we live in a world where things happen by chance, people would lose their bitterness and resentment. People could also see that believing that life inevitably gets worse after forty is a self-fulfilling prophecy, and that it is possible to lead a most satisfactory life at whatever age we are. People could choose to take responsibility for their bad temper. This should not be difficult because people would have already found that, in losing their resentment and fear, they would no longer be angry. Indeed, people would be happy or happier. Live all the days of your life!

Never Accept Defeat...Acknowledge and Forgive Yourself and Others

The verb "err" means to do something wrong; to make a mistake is "to err". "To err is human" because all people make mistakes. "To err is human, to forgive divine" says we should try hard to forgive others because all people are human and make mistakes. We include ourselves in "all people" who make mistakes so to forgive others when they make mistakes is the right thing to do. We must forgive ourselves as we proceed on our purpose driven journey.

Emotion rules differ depending on a person's cultural background (e.g., in some cultures the expression of anger meets with disapproval, in other cultures it is encouraged), they can also differ depending on a person's age (e.g., in Western cultures, the experience and expression of romantic love is considered more acceptable for young adults than for elderly people), gender (e.g., in Western cultures men are discouraged from expressing fear or sadness) and the social context (e.g., people typically express more anger towards family members than work colleagues). Your emotions impact your perception, cognition, and memory related to past social and personal relationships.

Emotional intelligence is the practice of engaging with others in a way which facilitates understanding of our own and others' emotions. Emotional intelligence helps your emotions to work for you instead of against you. Emotional intelligence is not a mere unleashing of the emotions, it is also learning to understand, manage and control them. Being emotionally competent means that you know how to manage your emotions, because you understand them. In his book, Emotional Intelligence with Heart, Claude Steiner's book explained, "Emotional intelligence training will help you to learn how to express your feelings, when and where to express them, and how they affect others. With training, you will become an emotional gourmand, aware of the texture, flavor, and aftertaste of your emotions. You will learn how to let your rational skills work hand-in-hand with your emotional skills, adding to your ability to relate to other people. Nurturing emotional intelligence helps people to recognize, understand, handle and appropriately express their emotions.

Forgiveness comes with our emotional intelligence in understanding ourselves and others. Forgiveness is a complex psychological and relational process that is more a discovery than an act of will. Forgiveness is associated with empathy and emotional intelligence. For example, marital and family therapists facilitate an empathic relational environment where ambivalence is expected and tolerated for enhancing the process of forgiveness. Relevant clinical cases are shared to illustrate the process of forgiveness as discovery.

Compassion and forgiveness operate on two levels. First, forgiveness in how we relate to ourselves, and second, forgiveness in how we relate to others. When we make mistakes, when our behavior fails to conform to universal human principles, we need to be able to treat ourselves with compassion and forgiveness so we can move forward to build our moral capacity. Learning from our mistakes should make us better persons by being kind, feeling deep feelings, letting these feelings go when needed, letting go of the need to be perfect, connecting with your inner peace and forgiving.

If we catch ourselves becoming angry by someone's carelessness, why not stop and forgive them? It's an opportunity to transcend our human limitations and act in a divine way. The purpose of forgiveness is not to absolve others, for who are we to judge them? Rather, the purpose is to free ourselves from the toxicity of resentment, animosity, and bitterness. Those who hold a grudge are held hostage by fear, guilt, and anger. It doesn't make sense to shackle ourselves to negative feelings and limiting beliefs. You should to choose forgiveness, or the path of peace, understanding, and acceptance. Forgiveness is an act of charity. Though, at first, it may seem a sign of weakness or self-loathing, it is in fact a sign of great power. When you earnestly forgive someone for their wrongdoing, you have set yourself above their harmful act. You are saying to them and to those around you "This is nothing. I am greater than this. This is not worthy of settling of score. This is trivial." All people as they say commit sins and make mistakes. God forgives them, and you are acting in a godlike (divine) way when you forgive.

Principles

- Trust is an emotional and you cannot find trust in someone else until you trust yourself, trust comes from within.

- Trust allows you to actually change your life without fear.

6
POSITIVE MULTI-DIMENSIONAL HEALING

"The battles that count aren't the ones for gold medals. The struggles within yourself—the invisible, inevitable battles inside all of us—that's where it's at."

— Jesse Owens, *Blackthink*

Healing Attitudes

My mother used to say, "You're going to have days that are not going your way but you have to be thankful for where you are although it's not where you want to be. Be thankful that you aren't where you used to be." Grim despair of the past is the past. All that matters now is the future. Reoccurring negative victimization thoughts about past events create strong emotions and unhealthy thinking which can generate unproductive feelings such as stress, anxiety, anger, guilt and depression. If you want to change how you feel and act, you must first change what you think. The biggest challenge to healing is within us, changing our attitude and thinking. Unhealthy thinking causes unhealthy emotions and attitudes, leading to unhealthy behavior. The antidote is healthy positive thinking. This means you have to keep changing your thoughts, attitudes and behaviors to keep yourself on track towards your dreams and goals. Thinking thoughts without action or movement is like having a dream without action, which is a nightmare. We need to change our thoughts and then put ourselves into motion and do something to initiate change and achieve our dreams. We need to heal and begin to live our dreams. If your current attitude isn't working, then develop a healing attitude and change it.

Disagreements occur in any relationship. Two people can not possibly always have the same needs, opinions and expectations. A relationship devoid of challenge stops growing and becomes routine, predictable, and hollow. But meeting the challenges of a relationship takes skilled communication. Part of the problem in developing a healing attitude that many of us were never taught how to understand and cope with our feelings in a healthy way, especially our emotional pain. That means that most people tend to believe in the three myths of coping with your feelings and emotional pain that most of us learned while growing up. The first, we should simply shake off any feelings we have and "get over it." The second, is to talk about our emotional pain and talking will make it go away. The third myth is that time heals all wounds. But there are too many of us carrying unhealed emotional hurts from the past.

Conflict in relationships is a deal breaker and a heart breaker but it is also the foundation of growth and trust. Conflict helps us heal, strengthen and shape productive and fulfilling relationships. If we can confront and resolve conflicts swiftly, without resorting to punishing criticism, contempt, defensiveness, or spacing out, our relationships will strengthen. Success or failure to resolve conflict hinges on our ability to apply the nonverbal skills that create an effective communication process.

Our minds have recovery powers to heal pain and stress, and recover peace and joy, by loosening the clinging attitudes called "holding onto the past." If we apply the mind's healing power, we can heal not only our mental and emotional concerns, but physical problems also. Happiness and success begins with our state of mind. If we maintain a favorable state of mind, we will ultimately get favorable results. If we carry a fault-finding state of mind and continue to carry baggage from the past, we will not be able to heal and continue to get similar comparable unfavorable results in life.

The first step towards dealing with stress is controlling your thoughts and the amount of stress you experience. In order to heal, you must look for clues, gathering information and putting it all together to make sense of what you learned from the situation. You need to explore at your own pace. Take the time to enjoy yourself. Begin with the sensory experiences that appeal most and take it from there. Amid your journey, look for sensory stimulants that provides relaxation and energy. Staying in touch with your emotional center is how you can stay connected to your core values. Consciously connecting your daily choices to your core values will help give you more peace, and balance in stressful situations. Caring for yourself builds stronger relationships and businesses and ultimately promotes more compassion. Healing begins within as you gain greater focus and ability to stay in touch with your emotional center by staying connected to your core values. This will help you to set your direction and keep your priorities clear. Take time to reflect, rest, relax, and integrate. The busyness epidemic in our culture is escalating, like a rapidly spreading disease. You should create the time for reflection, learning about what causes you stress and allowing for reorientation of your expectations and needs.

It is divine to forgive yourself and move on. Mishaps sometimes turn out to be the beginning of a new adventure or new career. You must make the most of happenstance in your life and career. Mistakes provide lessons and opportunities, if, you can find a way to take advantage of them. It is a better person for having gone through the experience of mishaps or mistakes. Now potential just seems like a bad word to you. You respect what hard work is now. Everything you have learned has helped prepare you for this day. In order to maneuver and prosper in your career despite unfortunate events or lost opportunities you must be able to overcome regrets, mistakes, and missed opportunities. We must overcome catastrophic thinking in order to be successful. Some people have an all-or-nothing way of thinking. People who spend their lives looking back over their shoulders in regret at what they didn't do are hindering their own success. Unless we are able to defend ourselves from our own negative internal dialogue, we risk failure. Research shows that people who give themselves positive reinforcement report an almost immediate improvement in their performance and an increase in energy.

In pursuing your dreams, you must take reasonable risks. Some people are just not risk takers, so they work for an organization where they're guaranteed a paycheck and they don't have to worry about layoffs, even though they are unhappy. You have to have the courage to be imperfect. Do you ask others for advice before making career decisions? Do you avoid projects at work that have the potential for failure?

You create your own luck. Almost everybody has had their life shaped by a series of unplanned events. You need to learn to take advantage of them and create events that will shape your lives, rather than waiting for them to happen. Waiting for opportunity to knock on your door doesn't work. You can take positive action to open up opportunities even when you don't know the outcome by making a list, of obstacles that you believe have limited your career progression so far. Go down the list and challenge each of the obstacles. You can keep your tools current by taking courses, attending seminars, and asking for growth assignments on your job and reading this book.

It is normal to make mistakes, including the type that hurts others. We probably have all made mistakes. And when we did so, we may have dismissed our mistakes with a simple, "Whoops, sorry about that, I'm only human, you know." Yes, we're only human; that's why pencils have erasers. But have you noticed when we are the victim of someone's mistake, we may become angry and hold it against them? In other words, if we make a mistake, it's because we're only human, but if "they" make a mistake, it's because they're stupid! Not rational, is it?

If you catch ourselves becoming angry by someone's carelessness, why not stop and forgive them? It's an opportunity to transcend your humanity and act in a great way. The purpose of forgiveness is not to absolve others, for who are we to judge them? Rather, the purpose is to free ourselves from the toxicity of resentment, animosity, and bitterness. Those who hold a grudge are held hostage by fear, guilt, and anger (Anger is one letter short of danger). It doesn't make sense to shackle yourselves to negative feelings and limiting beliefs. Isn't it much better to choose forgiveness, or the path of peace, understanding, and acceptance?

We find it hard to overlook peoples' mistakes. Are you still finding it difficult to forgive someone you know? We all have a story to tell because many of us have been injured psychologically to one degree or another. Perceiving an imagined threat, we snap at others. Not so with those we meet daily. Their injuries are psychological and hidden from view. As a result, we usually fail to realize their attacks are not due to viciousness, but to pain they have experienced.

So, the next time your friend, a family member, your supervisor or boss, spouse or significant other, or anyone else for that matter unfairly attacks you, don't get angry. Instead, pause, and imagine the situation differently. Would you get angry? How would you treat others if you knew in the past they had been hurt? Sometimes we are that person who has been hurt in the past, attacking others for no clear reason. At such a time, let's hope our victims will recognize us as a person who has been hurt or injured in the past and forgive us.

When we look at other people, we see many of their qualities in innumerable and other random combinations. However, the qualities that we see in the people around us are directly related to the traits that exist in us. "Like attracts like" is one of the spiritual laws of the universe. We attract individuals into our lives that mirror who we are. When you see beauty, divinity, sweetness, or light in the soul of another, you are seeing the goodness that resides in your soul. When you see traits in others that evoke feelings of anger, annoyance, or hatred, you may be seeing reflected back at you those parts of yourself that you have disowned or do not like. Often, the habits, attitudes, and behaviors of others are closely linked to our unconscious and unresolved issues. When you come into contact with someone you admire, search your soul for similarly admirable traits. Likewise, when you meet someone exhibiting traits that you dislike, accept that you are looking at your reflection. Looking at yourself through your perception of others can be a humbling and eye-opening experience. You can also cultivate in you the traits and behaviors that you do like. Be loving and respectful to all people, and you will attract individuals that will love and respect you back. Nurture compassion and empathy and let the goodness you see in others be your mirror.

Hatred can be irrational, and it has a greater impact on the individual who hates than the person or object being hated. Yet, overcoming hatred is difficult because hatred reinforces itself and causes greater enmity to come into being. The most powerful tool you can use to combat hatred is love. Deciding to love what you hate, whether this is a person, situation, or a part of yourself, can create a profound change in your feelings and your experience. There is little room for anger, dislike, bitterness, or resentment when you are busy loving what you hate. The practice of loving what you hate can transform and shift your emotions from hatred to love, because there is no room for hatred in a space occupied by love. Granted, it is difficult to forgo judging someone, love your enemy, and seek the good in situations that seem orchestrated to cause you pain or anger. On a simple level, loving what you dislike can help you enjoy your life more. On a more complex level, loving what you find objectionable sets you free because you disengage yourself from hatred that can weigh down the soul. Responding with love to people with hatred decreases their negative energy. You also empower yourself by not letting their negativity enter your personal space. Instead of reinforcing hatred, you become an advocate for love. Hatred responds to hate by causing anguish. But hatred responds to love by transforming into peace. Reflect compassion, empathy and be the change you want to see in the world.

We are reminded that we need to develop a healing attitude to help us with the problems in our lives. Many of us say we want to be accepted for being ourselves and for being the way we are, with all our frailties and weaknesses. If we do, then we must begin to really accept ourselves and others in the same way. Since we want to be forgiven and want people to forget all of our transgressions, failings, and misdeeds, we must learn to forgive and forget both ours and those of others.

We need to develop the power that will help us overcome our sense of guilt, over-responsibility, over-control, rescuing, and enabling others' problems. There are so many things in which we have no control and we must depend on our faith, beliefs and spirituality to help us.
We need to develop a new frame of reference that will help us keep our problems, anxieties, fears, and needs in perspective. We need to recognize that we are imperfect humans, prone to error, and not always strong enough to change. We must recognize our spirituality as the only power strong enough to handle all problems, anxieties, fears, and needs.

We need to develop a belief system that will help us gain the strength, understanding, confidence, and reassurance to let go of our grief, fears, over-responsibility, and guilt. We need to tap our spirituality whenever we need to handle a loss in our life. We need to develop a sense of hope to accept the things we cannot change, the courage to change the things we can, and the wisdom to know the difference. We need to develop altruistic love and giving so that we can make a difference in our lives and most importantly in other peoples' lives.

Smile With Your Eyes

Poor dental care can affect more than our mouth. Oral problems such as tooth loss, gum disease, stained teeth and bad breath can have a big impact on a person's confidence and overall happiness. Research has also found that people make judgments about a person's social and intellectual abilities based on whether or not they smile.

Increasingly, an alarming number of people are beginning to suffer needlessly from…too much seriousness. People are turning to anti-depressant medication. Depression medicines are expensive and they all have side effects. For those who say they want a no cost way to boost their spirits and improve their overall health without medical prescription, there is a solution.

Smile! Smiling reflects positive emotions, happiness and friendliness. Smiling isn't something we learn in the way that we learn to read and write, just look at how a baby smiles and laughs; it is pre-programmed behavior with which we are born. Smiling and laughing are just two of several natural stimuli which make the brains produce endorphins. Endorphins play a role in our body's defensive response to stress. Endorphins control emotions as well. When we are sad or mad, endorphins are released for re-elevating our emotions to glad. If fear strikes, endorphins allow coping by providing a feeling of calm euphoria. Diet, exercise, and general well-being control the production of endorphins, but stress and pain trigger their release which produces endorphins. It also increases the level of health-enhancing hormones like endorphins, and neurotransmitters. Laughter is very powerful medicine. When we laugh, natural killer cells important for our immune system which destroy tumors and viruses increase. Laughter lowers blood pressure and increases oxygen in the blood, which also encourages healing. Without humor our thought processes would become stuck and narrowly focused leading to increased distress. Just smiling can lower stress and dissolve anger by building bridges to other people around us.

Most of us think that a smiling person is a happy person, but how many of us know that just by smiling we can relieve stress and feel happier, even if for a moment. Of course, we have all heard the saying, "laughter is the best medicine." Behavioral Science studies do indicate a high positive correlation between humor and immune system benefits, but research has also shown smiling to be of benefit as well. Social psychology research bears out that facial expressions reflect our inner feelings, and changing our facial expression can help to change our feelings too. Research also shows that smiling produces the emotion most closely related to it, happiness. Laughter is good medicine and it all starts with a smile.

Starting today, you may want to laugh and smile as much as possible. As simple as it sounds, smiling and laughing causes chemical reactions in your body which are useful in improving your cardiovascular system, respiratory system, muscular system, central nervous system, and endocrine system.

Research shows that smiling and laughing can boost the immune system, helping the body to stay disease free and fight colds and the flu, and can help people with Type II diabetes process sugar after meals. A little smiling and laughing will help improve your health. If you are facing an illness, smiling, having a positive outlook and a sense of humor will keep your body open to healing. Take the time to smile, focus on the positive and be thankful for the good things in your life.

Life looks brighter when you look at them through smiling eyes. Drawing your face into a smile both by pulling the corners of your mouth upward and by squeezing your eyes can make you feel happier. In other words, we don't just smile because we feel happy; we can feel happy because we smile! When we smile we become more beautiful. Smiling warms the hearts of others and ours too. Replacing a miserable expression with a smile benefits everyone. So use this technique and you will smile naturally. Give me a smile! A smile begins with the eyes. You should resist smiling only with your mouth. When you smile with your eyes, it will spread and your mouth will move naturally and easily into a genuine smile. Let the smile with your mouth come naturally when it is ready. Beam with your eyes, and keep the rest of your face motionless until it breaks into a warm, friendly smile! Smile with your eyes! Smiling a full smile may impact more than our emotions; it may influence our general health.

Moving the face into the full smile can generate feedback loops that stimulate chemicals that tell the body and the brain that a certain emotion is being experienced, and then generate that emotion subsequently. Smiling, a full smile, may impact more than our emotions; it may influence our general health. For example, in men with heart disease, those with full smiles had less risk for potential damage to the heart muscle.

A smile and a sense of humor are good for your body, mind, and spirit. If we can learn to smile at ourselves we can bask in a warm, harmonizing energy that will penetrate our whole being and permeate our entire energy-system.

Studies show that positive effects of smiling occur whether the smile is fake or real. If you are facing an illness, having a positive outlook and a sense of humor will keep your body open to healing. If you are healthy, laughing will help to make sure you stay that way and can add to life enjoyment by serving as a tool to reduce your daily stress. Of course, it can be hard to keep a positive outlook all the time. But there are so many things out there to smile about and all you have to do is find one. The dance of life is always moving and it has its own rhythm and timing. You will be amazed at how much brighter things can become when you look at them through smiling eyes. So, even if you don't feel happy, rather especially if you don't, just smile! Make sure you squeeze your eyes as well as draw up the corners of your mouth. Do it right now, go ahead.

Nonverbal Emotional Communications

Most of the research into nonverbal communications shows that people are not very good at hiding their feelings. Facial expression, along with sight and perception, is core to how a message is perceived by the receiver. A look of disgust, happiness or remorse within a person's facial features can tell a lot about how someone is feeling without using words. Facial expression is always used in effective human communication. All through life, we are communicating via our facial expression, the eye contact we do or do not make, the cues our faces provide as to our mood. People look at our faces so that they can figure out how best to communicate with us and if we are listening to them. Smiling or signaling with your eyes that you are open and ready to make contact invites the other person to respond – in response, your look is returned and eye contact made. Smiling is an emotional expression which gives the impression that you are friendly, cheerful, easy-going, kind, likeable with a sense of humor, intelligent, well-adjusted. People smile for all sorts of reasons, to signal happiness, that you are approachable and ready for communication.

Smiles have a powerful effect on us. Smiling is a powerful cue that transmits happiness, friendliness, warmth, and liking. Smiling is often contagious and people will react favorably. They will be more comfortable around you and will want to listen to you more. Smiling is recognized across cultures as a sign of friendliness. However there are cultural and gender differences in nonverbal communication. For example, in some cultures, it is considered "forward" and inappropriate for women to show broad smiles.

Communication is the exchange and flow of information and ideas from one person to another. Many of the problems that occur in an organization are the direct result of people failing to communicate. Faulty communication causes the most problems. It leads to confusion and can cause a good plan to fail.

If you want to boost your spirits and your health with no prescription needed, then you want to laugh and smile as much as possible. As simple as it sounds, laughing and smiling, word allows you to get swept away with overall good humor, is beneficial to the cardiovascular system, respiratory system, muscular system, central nervous system and endocrine system. If you are facing an illness, having a positive outlook and a sense of humor will keep your body open to healing. If you are healthy, laughing will help to make sure you stay that way, and can add enjoyment to your work and home life and reduce your daily stress. Of course, it can be hard to keep a positive outlook all the time.

People do not see things the same way when under stress. What we see and believe at a given moment is influenced by our psychological frames of references - our beliefs, values, knowledge, experiences, and goals. If you are having a bad day or are feeling unhappy with the team project, you could be giving off negative signals with body language or a harsh tone. Even if you are saying the right thing, team members may still react negatively if you send the wrong body language signals. If you are feeling tense before going into a meeting, try taking a deep breath to relax.

Misunderstanding or missing nonverbal cues can cause serious problems in communications and in our relationships in general. So, facial expressions are important. Pay attention to your interactions to see if you frown or sigh. A sigh can make you seem disinterested. A frown can make you seem angry. If someone says something that surprises you or gives you the impression that they are uninformed, do you raise your eyebrows? This could be interpreted that you think they are stupid, even if that is not what you are thinking.

While trying to provide useful and hopeful information, make sure that your head is not shaking from side to side. Doing so is like a doctor making a diagnosis with his or her fingers crossed. We need to avoid giving mixed communications messages. Our words and our body language need to be congruent. We should limit our facial expressions to positive gestures, such as smiling which will help to give people less reason to question whether you and they are on the same side.

Significant research conducted in nonclinical settings has found gender differences in the way people communicate. The magnitude of gender differences in nonverbal expression rivals or exceeds the gender differences found for a wide range of other psychological variables. Compared with women, men have been shown to be less likely to engage in smiling, laughing and gazing at others. Men also tend to keep greater distances between themselves and others and exhibit weaker nonverbal communication skills than do women. People generally smile more at women than at men, which could affect communication. Because of these gender differences, men may have to work harder to achieve effective nonverbal communication, particularly with other.

We need to determine how effectively we communicate nonverbally and improve our interpret signals sent by others. Then, we need to practice overcoming any bad nonverbal habits until we become proficient in our body language skills. It is important to remember that all nonverbal communication is interpreted, correctly or incorrectly. The best way to minimize misinterpretation is to match our nonverbal communication with the impression we want to make.

Heightened awareness of the need to acknowledge peoples' nonverbal behavior should enrich your relationships with people and the quality of the gift you offer them. A simple smile can simulate good rapport and help create a sufficiently congenial and non-hostile atmosphere. It is important to smile, a friendly smile.

Live Cheerfully

Sometimes we all need encouraging words or to read positive-thoughts to help us on our inner journey. We can inject ourselves with energy and motivation by listening and reading to empowering thoughts. We are told that garbage-in garbage-out is still a universal law of nature. Stated another way: positive thought in, positive empowering thoughts out. We all have thoughts or feelings that, at some point, turn to actions. These actions that may be good, bad or neutral. Good actions are the rights actions to perform. Bad actions are the wrong actions performed. A neutral action sits you on the fence.

Quite often, we are bound by our religion, gender, age, culture and color which can dictate our thoughts, judgment and actions. The Law of Action and Reaction is similar to Newton's Law of Motion and states that, in our physical world, for every action there will be an equal and opposite reaction. The law of thoughts states that for every action, there will be an equal and opposite reaction in a spiritual rather than the physical sense. This means that when we give happiness, we receive happiness in return. From every thought, we act and will, we either enjoy or suffer the effects of that action. Yes, we shall have to suffer the consequences of our bad actions but we can equally reap the benefits of good performed. If we performed "pure" acts we create a better destiny. Thoughts are similar to seeds. Just as a seed will grow into a tree to bear flowers and fruits, actions will lead to inter-related actions to create a positive or negative situation.

We can benefit from developing an understanding of the Law of Thoughts. Understanding the Law of Thoughts helps us realize that we are totally responsible for our situations. Just as the understanding of Newton's Law of Motion has enabled us to benefit with our physical inventions, understanding the Law of Thoughts will help free us from the bondage of thoughts that lead to unhappiness and sorrow. Since thoughts can create unhappiness, we must avoid increasing our negative thoughts. Powerful thoughts are the actions we perform to fulfill our responsibilities as the instruments of the Creator, God.

We can influence our own happiness in small ways by attending to the moment. People should not measure their lives on the quality of their memories alone. Time is the most valuable resource we have. We should pay careful attention to how we spend our time. Well-being is a product of "focal time," or how we direct our attention. This is the key idea behind the different roles that pleasures and comforts have in creating happiness. Pleasures are stimuli that we give attention to: a good meal, a silky shirt, a boisterous evening with friends. If you ask someone with a very expensive car if he or she likes it, they'll probably say yes, since its high quality can bring happiness. Many of us are much too busy multitasking to pay attention to the expensive car's smooth ride, so at that moment the quality of the car hardly matters. So, are you better off if you are driving an economical car or an expensive one? At the same time, something, like getting flowers, will get your attention. Attention plays a role in the moment-by-moment experiences we call happiness. When asked some people may say they are happier with friends than when they are with a spouse or child. It sounds counterintuitive, but it makes sense: When we're with friends, we're intensely engaged, whereas we don't pay as much focused attention to family. They fade into the background, since we see them all the time. If we heed what does give us immediate pleasure, and if we are skeptical of our error-riddled memories and predictions, we can learn to focus our thought and begin to spend our money, time and attention in ways that make us happier. For, it is these moments that we remember.

We need to focus our mental consciousness and actions in ways that bring happiness to self and others. There is no limited amount of happiness. We can be happy this moment, an hour from now and into next year. We find happiness everywhere: in our beliefs, in our faith, our work, friends, family, self. We can gain an unlimited amount of happiness from them all.

Your personal style helps you choose career goals and environments that allow you to perform well and be content. For instance, some people need settings where they have lots of time for quiet concentration. Others thrive on a combination of quiet time and interaction with other people. Your personal style will help you choose your preferred environment. Values are the core principles that should determine what you do, who you spend your time with, and how you think about the world. Knowing your values is crucial for making wise life choices. And when you choose a career that reflects your priorities, you will feel more committed to what you are doing and will be more satisfied in your environment. As my mother used to say, you've got to be something before you can do something. Self awareness is the key.

Many of us think that if only we had lots of money we could do what we want and then we would be happy. Happiness does not depend on future events or possessions. Happiness can come from within. You can love yourself and love your life today. Each individual approaches life in a unique way. Differences in self-expression can be attributed to how you value creativity, independence, excitement and personal development. Your values in these areas will influence both the types of activities and lifestyle environments that you will find enjoyable and satisfying. All of your values may not be met in your career. One of the secrets of effective career management is finding other ways to fulfill your values which are not being met in your career. Many values can be satisfied in other areas, such as volunteer work, recreational pursuits and participation in groups or clubs. We can begin by choosing our attitude to life and not make our happiness dependent upon future circumstances.

Having self-awareness and cultural awareness gives us all, regardless of our culture, a sense of identity and core values that allows us to function more successfully in both our personal and professional lives. Equally important, however, is that knowing our own culture makes it possible to more accurately interpret the needs and behaviors of colleagues, customers or clients. Because of this assumption that values are universal, we tend to assume that everyone is doing what they are doing for the same reasons we would. Our values and of the fact that they are not necessarily shared by everyone we meet. Once we realize that our views are not human nature, we are in a far better position to accurately interpret the motivations and needs of those around us.

How often do you ask yourself, who am I really? Asking is the first step. Knowing yourself is the second step. Without knowing yourself, you have no basis for thinking. You will get caught up in illusions: material, business, career, status, political, religious, and other endless illusions. Knowing yourself is one of the most challenging and important tasks of your life. If you know who you are and what you want, you will have a better chance of figuring out how to achieve your own success, happiness and personal fulfillment.

Before you can achieve any goals in life you have to know how to set them. Before you can set your goals you need to decide what is important to you, what your values are. There are no right or wrong values, they can be anything that you consider important or maybe something that you couldn't imagine living without. Just make sure that the values you choose to define yourself are truly your own values and not someone else's. If you value knowledge you should structure a lifestyle where you are constantly learning. If you love to be surrounded by beauty, open your eyes to the beauty all around you. If recognition is what you want, you first have to choose what you want to be recognized for. Remember to choose something that you have a talent in. If family is important to you. Family can mean many things. It can be people that you are related to or just a group of people that you are close to. If you enjoy adventure. Remember you can have a little of everything in moderation. Whatever you value, it is important, it means that you are proud of yourself and your values, no matter how they look in somebody else's eyes. Envision your future and choose a professional and personal life that you feel is worthwhile.

To know yourself is to clarify your gifts, your talents, your life challenges and how you experience your personality and soul. The more you know and express your authentic self, the more you will smile, the more meaning, joy and fulfillment you will have in your life. We all know by now that change is inevitable but we are slow to learn that growth is intentional and it requires a lot of action on our part. Therefore, we need to create a clear growth path for ourselves. To become more authentic and bona fide and genuine and real so that we can respond to reach our potentials.

For too long, too many of us have been stuck in neutral going no where, procrastinating by saying we want balance, peace of mind and success but taking no action. This is the beginning of a new day, now is the time to make the most of your life. The first step is to find out what is behind our procrastination, busyness and perfection and then take time out to create discipline to rest and be aware of our cause and effects. We need to experience real free time, peace of mind and success by setting meaningful goals, managing our time better, staying on track and getting more done more easily. The key is to accomplish what's most important first and stay organized and focused.

There is an old saying, the more you know, the more you know you don't know. The more you understand and know about who you are; you gain self appreciation and your levels of self-acceptance increases, while your negativity decreases along with many of your fears and anger. On the positive side, your self esteem will improve dramatically, your courage will increase and you will have increased hope and joy. As you increase in knowing who you are, our ability to identify as a victim decrease, you gain increased power on issues around us including your finances and money. Simply reading this far, you are now able to Identify and replace limiting beliefs that stop you from experiencing abundance.

If you have feelings of emptiness, or meaningless and you want your life to have more purpose. Remember, you're not alone. Most people don't know and don't know they don't know, so you have a head start on most people trying to grow. Just, knowing your life purpose and fully living it brings much meaning and fulfillment into your life. When we consciously align with our deepest reasons for being, we tap into our rich reserves of energy, personal power and passion. Our lives will begin to flow in new and delightful ways.

Believe in yourself, live your values and success will be yours! If you don't make a million, you will make yourself a better person anyway. Learn to be a human being, become a human doing and you'll end up as a human enjoying the lifestyle you deserve as a result of being true to yourself. Put yourself in action, whatever the outcome, live cheerfully.

Be Calm

Stress is a part of life and is often unseen. The first step in handling stress is identifying source. You may have experienced some of these changes as fear. Adrenaline comes to the rescue and causes a number of changes that help us to survive. Adrenaline also shuts down all functions of the body not needed in an emergency. Digestion, sexual function, even the immune system is temporarily turned off. If necessary, excess waste is eliminated by urination and diarrhea. Where speed and physical strength are important, adrenaline stress will be helpful and beneficial. Fear can help us to survive or perform better.

Survival stress may occur when your survival or physical integrity is threatened. Stress can be internally generated. It can also come from an 'addiction' to and enjoyment of stress. Your personality can affect the way in which you experience stress. You may be familiar with the idea of 'type A' personalities who thrive on stress, and 'type B' personalities who are mellower and more relaxed in their approach. Other aspects of personality can cause stress. Perfectionism, where the perfectionist's extremely or impossibly high standards can cause stress. Stress influences the way that we think. Stress increases based on how we think about events and circumstances. Some folks tend to exagerate the severity events, making mountains out of molehills, or exaggerating the consequences. They tend to react to small things with larger than warranted feelings, exaggerating the event to match their feelings, rather than adjusting their feelings to the event. People with low stress tolerance tend to make molehills out of mountains.

Anxiety occurs when you are concerned that circumstances are out of control. Many of the stresses you experience may come from your job or from your lifestyle. Stress results from having to overcome unnecessary obstacles, time pressures and deadlines, changes in procedures and policies, lack of support and advice, lack of clear objectives, unclear expectations of your role on your job or relationships. Stress can get into a vicious circle of stress, which causes you to hurry jobs and do them badly. This under-performance causes feelings of frustration and failure, which causes more stress, which causes more hurry and less success. Stress-creating behavior can compound this, as can an inability to relax and affect your health.

No doubt, change can be stressful. It is important that we learn to welcome change, otherwise we can expose ourselves to intense stress. As some companies experienced with the industrial revolution, people who resist change will be crushed by it. Your success depends on adaptation to, or anticipation of, change.

Our families can be a source of stress. Families are a complex network of interactions. Each personality affects the entire system. An alcoholic in the family disrupts the system and often leads to the system trying to adapt to the resulting dysfunction. Sometimes that adaptation creates difficulties as well.

Relationships can be stressful. A primary relationship is often stressful. Each person in the relationship brings expectations, a set of explicit implicit and unrealistic expectations. These expectations, when in conflict with the other person's expectations, can create a great deal of conflict; and this conflict is stressful.

Our social environment can cause stress due to insufficient working and living space, noise, and pollution. A badly organized or run down environment is stressful. The food we eat may contribute to the stresses we experience. However, our body reacts to correct disease: abnormally high sugar levels from too much insulin, too much salt, not enough sleep. Chemical imbalances can raise or lower our blood pressure, cause liver, digestive and other malfunctions. Some may experience stress from an unbalanced or unhealthy diet. We may find that dietary deficiency or excess caloric causes discomfort and illness which generates stress. Obesity causes not only physical stress but internal organ and emotional stress. It can become a vicious cycle of cause and effect.

Puberty are severe stressors, a person's body actually changes shape, sexual organs begin to function, and new hormones are released in large quantities. For women past puberty, a lack of female hormones is a major stress on the body. Once a month, just prior to menstruation, a woman's hormone levels drop sharply. Following a pregnancy, hormone levels change dramatically. At another point in a woman's life hormone levels decline enough to produce overstress.

Increasingly, we suffer from work stress. Do you face conflicting demands? Do you deal with excessive job requirements - tasks and assignments that clearly exceed your ability or training? Do you lack job security? Do you have an inflexible work environment? Does hard work earn reward? Conflicts on the job, dissatisfaction with one's supervisor or with the job itself, insufficient financial compensation, job insecurity, fear of changing a job for greater advancement, feeling stifled in a quest for power, not feeling appreciated or acknowledged, all produce significant stress. The degree of your stress will vary depending your personality. Stresses you experience from your job may include time pressures and deadlines; changes in procedures and policies; lack of relevant information, support and advice; unclear expectations of your role from your boss or colleagues;

responsibility for people, budgets or equipment; career development stress such as under-promotion, frustration and boredom with current role; over-promotion beyond abilities; lack of a clear plan for career development; lack of opportunity; and lack of job security.

A particularly unpleasant source of stress comes from the "hurry sickness." We can get into a vicious circle, which causes us to hurry jobs or do them badly. Stress-creating behavior compounds our inability to relax at home or on holiday. If we do not manage long term stress effectively, it can lead to long term fatigue, failure and one of the forms of physical or mental illnesses. We can neutralize stress by effective use of stress management techniques. The strategies that we should adopt to manage stress depends on the source.

You can develop stress resource lists which can help us get feedback from the subconscious about what is important for you. You can use stress management resources to stimulate your thinking and create new inner connections. Calm is about being at peace with yourself so that you are able to cope with life and its ups and downs. During a stressful day, our blood pressure may rise. Stress and anxiety can lead to depression, insomnia, lack of concentration, anger, cancer, fear, migraine, physical pain, loss of self-esteem, and lead to bad habits like smoking and weight gain. Many of today's challenges commence with stress. Stress and stress related illnesses push many people to an earlier than necessary grave.

When your mind, on an emotional level, is disturbed for the moment, you may not actually discern reality though, because of the negative emotion in that period. That's the nature of stress. Therefore, a calm mind is essential. But achieving a calm mind, is not through knowledge alone you will need compassion, a sense of forgiveness, a sense of tolerance. These will give you inner strength. With inner strength comes more self-confidence. And with that comes less fear, less doubt; you can see objectively because you have self-confidence. Calmness, serenity and peace are the result of your time-consuming and patient effort to achieve more self-control over your lives. You become happier, calmer and at peace when you understand yourselves as a thinking evolved, reflective person. You gain the knowledge necessary to understand other people as the result of your thought, and as you develop the right understanding. As you begin to see more clearly the internal relations of things by the action of cause and effect, you become happy, calm and at peace. You will cease to waste your time fussing and fuming and worrying and grieving. You will remain poised, resolute in your happiness, peace and serenity.

Even if you label ourselves an ordinary person, you will find your prosperity increase as you develop greater self-control and develop more calmness. We all know that people always prefer dealing with a person whose demeanor is calm and levelheaded. We also understand that the strong, calm person is always loved and revered.

Who does not love a tranquil heart, a sweet-tempered and balanced life? Peace and serenity are precious as wisdom, more to be desired than material things such as expensive jewelry, big house, fine clothes and such, even more than fine gold. How insignificant mere money-seeking and materialism looks in comparison to a peaceful life.

No matter what you want to achieve or cope with in life, you can make it easier for yourselves if you deliberately use the power of your deeper inner mind. Imagine a life that dwells in the ocean of genuineness and understanding, beneath the waves, beyond the reach of conflict, tension, envy, jealousy, anger and hatred. The law of cause, and effect or karma says, "Every cause has its effect; every effect has its cause; everything happens according to law. Chance is but a name for law not recognized; there are many planes of causation, but nothing escapes the law." Webster defines the word "chance" as, "A supposed agent or mode of activity other than a force, law or purpose; the operation or activity of such agent; the supposed effect of such an agent; a happening; fortuity; casualty, etc." According to the Law of Cause and Effect, nothing happens by chance, chance is merely a term indicating cause existing but not recognized or perceived, that phenomena is continuous and without break or exception. For example, nothing will bring serenity into our life, unless you do something such as seeking to understand who you are, become at peace with who we are and practice being at peace with yourselves and others.

Our reaction emotionally to changes and experiences develops our understanding and wisdom. With each emotional reaction, your awareness, comparison, thoughts and feelings evolve. You can transcend our past experiences by acting with awareness and understanding. You can analyze history for numerous examples such as Mahatma Gandhi who was physically frail but his heart and karuna, made him a popular powerful leader. Compassion automatically brings happiness and calmness. Hatred, jealousy and excessive attachments cause suffering and agitation. It is compassion that can help you overcome hatred, jealousy and excessive attachment to material and meaningless things and move you into a calm state of mind.

Compassion is a virtue, a disposition or temperament to make certain kinds of choices, and not simply an emotion. It is easy for many to be compassionate with our friends but it can and must be extended beyond friends to encompass strangers. Compassion is not just being kind to your friend. That is attachment because it is based on expectation. Compassion is giving loving recognition, not only to those around you but also to people you dislike, and your enemies. Karuna or compassion flows towards all of our emotions, feelings, reactions and attitudes and presents itself as kindness especially towards those who are suffering.

We must understand and keep in mind that developing karuna might not benefit another person or others directly. If you try to develop karuna towards your enemy, your enemy might not even be aware of it. You develop karuna by calming your mind. On the other hand, if you keep thinking how awful everything is, you will immediately lose your peace of mind. It is not necessarily so much helping your enemy but when you lose your peace of mind, you are actually harming yourself. And that in itself helps your enemy. By changing your thoughts, you immediately get inner peace.

Surprisingly, many people also think that the practice of karuna benefits others and not oneself. Even modern medical researchers have come to the conclusion that peace of mind is vital to good health. Health studies and experiments show that it is easier for those who practice love and compassion to regain a peaceful state of mind after being agitated. This goes to prove that the practice of compassion actually calms you down. It is part of the "secular ethics." There is nothing sacred or religious about aspiring to a calm mind. My approach promotes values that enable me and others I meet on my journey to have a calm mind.

Having a calm mind actually works wonders. It is important to encourage all people, especially young people to realize that if you lose your temper, you will suffer. If we smile, life becomes sweeter. After all, it has been proven, if you smile at another person, they will smile back! Everyone has experienced anger. If you let anger remain within you, it leads to ill-feeling and hatred and may affect your health in the long run. Negative emotions are part of your mind and that is why compassion is so important.

I am convinced that we must keep the past in the past, not let little disputes injure great relationships. Remember that both great love and achievement involve great risks. The goal in life is to improve your life and to achieve all of your dreams. With that as a goal, compassion is the key to having a calm mind in living your life dreams and working wonders. I wish that you live and enjoy a life of calmness, serenity and peace and that you live in joy forever.

Persistence and Willpower

We are often reminded that change is not easy and changing the way we live is even harder. We also understand that many of us have adopted some of our bad habits to make up for imbalances in other parts of our life. For example, you want to lose weight but reward yourselves with sweets or ice creams at the end of the day because our work is so stressful. You know that sweets are aggravating or perpetuating one your major health complaints but you eat anyway. You are actually shooting yourselves in the foot. In other words, your health problem may contribute to causing your workday to be stressful. Sweets may be perpetuating your weight problem and some of your stress of the day may come from constantly feeling insecure about yourselves because we're overweight. The more insecure you feel, the easier it becomes to get caught in vicious cycles like this.

What can we do? We might have to eschew the sweets and take herbs or enzymes instead. When we get this right, we may have fewer cravings, and it'll be easier to eliminate the sweets. Although it isn't easy, we still have to make that decision and stand by it.

History teaches us that change requires clarity, willingness and discipline. This is a major obstacle to better health for all of us and a better world. Without these three qualities, we are at the mercy of our own unhealthy cravings and obsessions. These cravings may give us short term comfort, but in the long run, they lead only to disease and death.

- Without clarity, we don't know we need to change.
- Without willingness, we cannot adopt better habits.
- Without discipline, we cannot keep from falling back into the old habits.

According to Chinese medicine physiology, internal organs are attacked by the internal causes such as the emotions of excitement or joy, sympathy, grief, fear or shock and anger. Many problems begin with relationships and emotions. This includes arrogance, affection, obsession, lack of concentration, forgetful, difficulty with giving and receiving, very sensitive, distrust, and shyness; despair, gloom, discouragement, hopelessness, nervousness, and self-doubt. Worry, even with a smooth exterior, will break through and you will break down, disease will claim you. People who carry a burden of worry become enervated and lose health. The cause of their worry is lack of control of eating, lack of control of the emotions, lack of care of the body, and lack of efficiency. Instead of resolutely going to work to remove all the defects, you are downed by them. An uncontrollable temper must be downed, or it will down the one who gives way to it. For example, a very intelligent person may be able to verbalize knowledge, but may find it difficult to translate that knowledge into practical action.

The internal organs are also affected by unhealthy food and a bad lifestyle. We have to make decisions to change our health, and if we don't persist in our changes, nothing gets better. The following are illustrations of physiology and psychology of decision making and decision keeping:

- Perception, Clarity, and Calm: The Heart-system is not only a blood pumper, but also relates to our overall consciousness. If we have a problem here, our perception of life, of ourselves, and of our habits may be distorted. Heart-system problems most often show up as anxiety and insomnia, so you may have to deal with these first. Certain imbalances can obstruct clarity, or create mental and emotional unrest. Once you have more calm and clarity from the remedies in those areas, it will be easier to deal with other problems.

- Organizing and Categorizing Your Options: The spleen-system digests not only foods, but also ideas, concepts, etc. Once we have perceived our lives and our habits, then we analyze and categorize them. This requires energy, so if you have trouble with digestion, worry, or low energy, this part of the decision making process will be more difficult. In fact, even discussing issues may be hard to digest! Herbs, enzymes, different food choices, etc. will help you here, and then it'll be easier to deal with other problems in your life.

- Evaluating the Good and Bad: Some African and Chinese medicine authorities maintain that the small intestine is involved with separating good from bad options but this may also involve the spleen, heart, kidney and bladder. People have trouble distinguishing good and bad options for a number of reasons; you may lack the heart's clarity, or the spleen's strength. The answers relating to your specific patterns regarding anxiety, insomnia, and depression may involve you spleen, heart, kidney or bladder. Although you can certainly make philosophical arguments about how much gray there is in the world, decisions are much easier when you take a black and white perspective. In other words, you do one of two things: build health or produce disease in yourself.

- Making A Decision: After you have analyzed your options and decided which is best, you must make a decision. The most important organ for decision is the gallbladder. Gall is not just physiological bile (part of the digestive process), but also a psycho-emotional quality. You've probably heard it used of someone who was thought to be overly assertive: "Can you imagine- the gall!" Our oldest medical sourcebook, the Nei Jing, says, "The gallbladder is, like a judge in the imperial court, the one that decides." The Gallbladder is the organ that endows an individual with the ability to resolve, make decisions, and settle on a resolution. In the case where the gallbladder is abundant, decision-making ability is firm. In the case where the gallbladder is empty, the individual loses the capacity to decide; determination wanes; it transforms into fear, cowardice, and indecision. In the everyday language of China, it is said that a person with a small gallbladder (Dan Xiao) is shy, fearful, and cowardly, whereas a person with a large Gallbladder (Dan Da) is bold, intrepid, brave, and daring. The state of the gallbladder is proportional to the individual's force of character. As it has been written, No pain, no palm; no thorns, no throne; no gall, no glory; no cross, no crown. Make up your mind to act decidedly and take the consequences. No good is ever done in this world by hesitation. The first step to getting the things you want out of life is this: decide what you want. As you become more clear about who you really are, you'll be better able to decide what is best for you, the first time around. If you choose not to decide, you still have made a choice. Every oak tree started out as a nut who decided to stand its ground. The doors we open and close each day decide the lives we live. To decide, to be at the level of choice, is to take responsibility for your life and to be in control of your life.

- Persistence and Willpower: Persistence, not skill, is the one quality, the one personal characteristic that is the most highly correlated with success, whatever the field. To be successful, we need persistence. Determination is the will to endure to the end, to get knocked down fifty times and get up off the floor saying, here comes number fifty-one! After you've made your decision, you must persist with dogged will. Without persistence or willpower, there is no change. Actually, in the larger context of humanity, without willpower, nothing can be achieved. If we are completely subject to our whims, we are like children, we want what we want when we want it; we're unable to subjugate our desires, and we're incapable of paying now and playing later. The kidney-system is responsible for our willpower. It includes the adrenal glands, which produce cortisol, a natural steroid hormone that gives us a burst of intense strength. It's the source of the strength of the proverbial super mom who can lift the car that's sitting on her child. The Chinese said the essence of the Kidney is the Zhi, or Will.

According to Chinese writings, Zhi contains, "the emotion of self preservation, but also prudence and attentiveness." The kidneys are also associated with Kong and Jing, which mean fear and fright. When we are scared we go into a stress reaction that involves the release of cortisol from the adrenals. On the disease side, the Will (Zhi) can turn into recurring phobias, nervousness, and panic. But, Kong or fear can also be normal and useful in the form of "caution, fear of the unknown, and danger signals. For example, at times when we are rock climbing and about to make a risky move, feel some fatigue while taking risks, or suddenly get scared, we get a burst of cortisol along with a certain amount of caution. Some extremists ignore these danger signals and end their careers dead. We should always listen to the kidney's warnings and make a decision about whether or not the risk is manageable and worthwhile. It's not always easy to make rational decisions with a bunch of cortisol in your veins, so when we lean toward not taking the risk, we oscillate between thoughts of dealing with a dead or broken body, and insecurity feelings that we're not daring enough. The latter, of course, are irrational, and we know that because we're not limited by irrational fears.

One of the reasons we are so fascinated with successful professional athletes is that they seemed to be able to will a win and make it happen, to "put the rope in their teeth and drag themselves or their team across the finish line or score the winning point." But few of us would want to be make that much commitment for success.

As Aesop or Confucius might say, "it does not matter how slowly you go so long as you do not stop." Most of us have learned that this quote was true for the trudging, the arduous journey. All of our lives, we have been more of a sprinter. Then a long distance runner gives us something to do and we want to get it done quickly and then relax. In our younger days, we preferred to run the hundred-yard dash than the mile. We just thought the long runs were too painful. Little did we know that persistence is like a muscle, and it will become atrophied if not used. This is where your willpower comes in. Just imagine yourself as someone who was undisciplined earlier in life, someone who loved to sleep in, to indulge yourself, to revel in selfishness. But you are determined to improve yourself, to experience whatever human beings can experience, to prevail. Some of that comes from the conviction of our faith, that doing things consistent with our faith is the most important thing in life. Some of it comes from anger, our unwillingness to be the loser. And a little bit comes from ego, but less and less over time.

We have heard the story about the old mule that fell into a dry well. As the story goes, the farmer didn't think the mule or the dry well were worth saving. So, he decided to bury the mule in the well and put him out of his misery. Initially, the poor old mule was in a panic! But, as the shovel full of dirt struck his back...the mule began to...shake it off and step up. Each time the dirt hit, he would shake it off and step up. It wasn't long before the old mule, battered and exhausted, shook off that last shovel full of dirt and stepped triumphantly out of the well. What seemed to bury the old donkey, actually blessed him...all because of his persistence amidst the dirt. He was able to shake it off and step up! Maybe this is what it really means to hang in there. If we endure despite our difficulties and refuse to allow panic, bitterness, or self-pity control us, the obstacles that appear to bury us could actually become part of our success and richer blessings. Be yourself, be your best self persistently and you will end up making a difference in yourself, your mental and physical health, and the world.

Friendship and Love

You need to strengthen your friendship with your love ones by developing emotional intelligence through relationship enhancements. There are many sayings about friendship and love:

- Love starts with a smile, grows with a kiss, and ends with a tear.
- Don't cry over anyone who won't cry over you.
- Good friends are hard to find, harder to leave, and impossible to forget.
- Actions speak louder than words and words can cause a pain that last a lifetime so think before you act but don't forget to act.
- The hardest thing to do is watch the one you love, love somebody else.
- Life's short, a best friend is like a four-leaf clover: hard to find and lucky to have.
- If you think that the world means nothing, think again.
- Friends are forever. True friendship never ends.
- Don't frown. You never know who is falling in love with your smile.
- Remember, nobody is perfect until you fall in love with them.
- Most people walk in and out of you life. But true friends leave footprints in your heart.

When we look back on these days or our younger years, we will remember the people who supported our dream and passion when it wasn't popular, the people we went to school with the people who made us laugh, the people who hung out with us when nobody else would, and the people who made our lives better simply by being a part of it.

Don't wait for tomorrow for tomorrow one day will not come. This is the beginning of a new day; always appreciate the friends that you have. So send a "Thank you my friend" message or another special message to your friends and let them know that they are always loved and cared about.

Imagination and Creativity

Increasingly, the new core competence is creativity and imagination, the right brain. Imagination is more important than knowledge. Knowledge is limited; imagination is everywhere. Imagination is the "big picture," insight-oriented and favors inductive reasoning. Like creativity, imagination is grounded in our accumulated knowledge, and we all have imagination and creativity. It is, however, more than a combination of stored materials. The imagination serves us in many different ways. When we become depressed, we are imagination-deprived, our imagination has totally failed us. The results of our imaginations as well as the great imaginations of others can be seen everywhere and encourages progress. As it has been often quoted, "We stand on the shoulders of giants." Imagination challenges the status quo. Imagination is essential to learning.

Imagination (imagery) is the most fundamental language we have. Everything you do, the mind processes through images. When we recall events from our past or childhood, we think of pictures, images, sounds, pain, etc. Images aren't necessarily limited to visual but can be sounds, tastes, smells or a combination of sensations. Similarly, going to a place where you had a bad accident may instantly invoke visions of the accident and initiate flight or fight response. The lemon's tart aroma is overwhelming. Imagery is the language that the mind uses to communicate with the body. Imagery is the biological connection between the mind and body.

Imagery has been considered a healing tool in many cultures. Navajo Indians, for example, practice an elaborate form of imagery that encourages a person to "see" himself as healthy. Ancient Egyptians believed that images release spirits in the brain that arouse the heart and other parts of the body. Affirmations and visualizations are used by athletes everyday. It has been suggested by experts such as Dale Carnegie, Robert Schuller and Steven Covey to elicit peak performance in individuals. Athletes use visualization to enhance their performance, sometimes without realizing it. Tiger Woods may form a mental map of the fairway, imagining precisely where he will place the ball on each shot; a high jumper may visualize every split second of his approach to and leap over the bar; a baseball pitcher may run a mental film of the ball from the time it leaves his hand until it lands in the catcher's glove. Imagery is very powerful and crosses many disciplines. You can create an internal "comfort zone." This is extremely useful in mind body healing. You can use imagery as relaxation techniques designed to release brain chemicals that act as your body's natural brain tranquilizers, lowering blood pressure, heart rate, and anxiety levels. Because imagery relaxes the body, doctors specializing in imagery often recommend it for stress-related conditions such as headaches, chronic pain in the neck and back, high blood pressure, spastic colon, and cramping from premenstrual syndrome. Everyone can successfully use imagery. It's just like learning to play a music instrument or learning to fly an airplane. It is the same with imagery. You practice, practice and practice.

Too many of us remain one-tracked, instinctual and one-dimensional limiting our imagination and our ability to experience more love, create more beauty, manifest more results, change our conditions, rewrite our past, and connect to our purpose. As it has been written, we see things; and we say, why? But we dream things that never were; and we say, why not? Our imagination is a tool of freedom and provides us with the opportunity to try something new, new qualities and perspectives in our life. Through imagination, we can explore our past, problems, patterns, processes, plans, perceptions, principles, passions and purpose to uncover new possibilities.

Creative thinking is drawing upon greater potential within you, making and communicating connections to: think of many possibilities (imagery); think and experience in various ways and use different points of view; think of new and unusual possibilities (Imagination); and guide in generating and selecting alternatives. Life is a dream. Whatever is imaginable is possible. Great change comes when we become aware of the thoughts we are thinking moment by moment and re-frame them to produce the reactions we want. By becoming hyper-conscious of what we are thinking, we can also change our past by changing our beliefs. Looking at the past becomes helpful only to find the beliefs we formed that may not be serving us.

Possibility thinking is at the heart of creativity, and can be seen as involving the intersecting elements of people, processes and domains. It involves problem finding as well as problem solving, and involves the shift from "what is this" to "what can I/we do with this?" Your dreams are what are meant to be, you just have to do your part... a mighty tall order when you don't fully understand what your part is, nor the processes that make dreams come true. People who rise to the top of their field aren't just good at their jobs, they're affable, resilient, optimistic and have imagination.

Juggling Adversely Affects Learning and Memory

The best thing we can do to improve our memory is to pay attention to the things we want to remember. Tasks that require more attention will be adversely affected by multi-tasking.

The art of juggling, especially for women includes business or professional working, household duties, marriage or significant other commitments, parenthood, spiritual wellness, new learning and relationships in general. However, by its nature, mixed leadership programming generally does not address women's ways of thinking, learning, and leading. We live in a world that often focuses on the importance of making money. For many people, it has become their obsession...but for many of us, we have a stronger inner need, a desire for spiritual enlightenment is stronger. If you are reading this book, do you think it is by accident? There are no accidents in life, your life has a purpose and so does this time sensitive message.

The purpose of this book is to introduce you to something that will lead you along a beautiful pathway to a successful life. By reading this book, you are going to get more life-changing strategies and personal power than you will ever get from any other self-help book in that you read this year. My success and the hundreds of people I have successfully coached resulted from applying tools which I developed based on life lessons. You have the power to live happier than you ever imagined. This book will give you a warm feeling of assurance as if you've finally found what your soul has been searching for all these years. You'll experience a calm "knowing" that comes from somewhere deep inside of you and all fear will disappear.

We are sabotaging our potential for change. A part of you may want to grow and change, but another part may be resisting because change always moves you into new territory in your thinking and emotions. If you find you are getting anxious, fearful, angry, frustrated, dismissive or unmotivated, then defense mechanisms are at work. Just imagine that feeling of knowing what lies ahead is total success in all areas of your life. There are two ways to live your life. You can be your own advocate by acting on your dreams with results or you can sit on the sidelines as life passes you by trying to please other people. Work in general is never done, which is a good thing really, because if there is no more work to be done, there is no more progress to be made. But constant work without play makes for a very dull existence. The key to living life is balance. I believe there are four key areas of our lives that require (yes, require!) daily attention. Focus on your spirituality by taking time to center yourself and become more grounded in your faith, your core beliefs, whatever your interpretation of God may be. Be grateful and thankful and find quiet time to meditate and contemplate. This will help maintain your overall health. It does not matter what religion you practice, it matters only that you make time to honor your spiritual self and your connection to the Divine, every single day. First thing in the morning is best for most people, since it can help you adopt a positive mindset for your day. Some prefer the late evening hour before bedtime, to help de-stress their day. Each of us need time every day to work on our physical and emotional wellness. This is time we can use for exercise, keep a journal, self-explore, and do leisure activities. Again, it does not have to be massive amounts of time, but at least some time for exercise and self-care is necessary. Make yourself a priority, and make time to care properly for yourself, physically and emotionally. Here are some ways to help that. Have a "family day" or "family night" where you spend one evening or perhaps one weekend day together doing something fun as a family - and this doesn't include camping out around the television. Time spent together having fun is the most important thing. For couples, have a weekly "date night" where the two of you spend time alone together, without the kids, and without distraction. Work or business is last on my list. If you are not wealthy, you have to have a business or work. Most people today put work first and forget the rest, but doing so creates a sense of constant duty and drudgery. Work is important, but it's not the most important thing in life. If you make the other three categories your first priorities, your time spent working will be much more productive, you will be fully present in every moment, giving proper attention to every task. This means that at any given time, we are performing multiple tasks at the same time. Some we are performing with our hands and others in our mind.

I would ask the same questions you are probably asking yourself. Was I meant to struggle in life? Why was I not able to create this in my life before now? Everything takes practice. Before being fully committed, I would practice the techniques which I am about to share with you and have had great success with them. We plan and schedule; we write down and underscore; we promise and make resolutions; we organize and reorganize. But old habits are hard to break, we start out with success in planning, we accomplish a short lived time out from procrastination, and then return back to it. The problem of procrastination is one that often goes beyond self-discipline and whipping yourself from stasis to stress. It is usually the symptom of a multifaceted set of problems that defy a single solution. I use to be one of the biggest culprits of procrastination and it was hindering my life. Procrastination has a way of ruling our lives if we do not bring it under control. I figured the only way to fight my situation was to learn more about it. My procrastination was motivated by fear. First, I identified the source the sources of my fear, their effects on my self-esteem, and I dealt with the problems. Second, I got myself an appointment book, a simple one. The appointment book helped me to address the problems of disorganization and even poor memory. I had to learn to use it every day, writing down things you are going to do or that you have already done. I used it to look ahead into the next week, not next year. You can write in important telephone numbers and addresses as you acquire them. You can carry it around with you all day and make it a habit. You can use it to learn how to plan ahead realistically by break down tasks into tangible stage goals, and provide these goals with appropriate deadlines. Then you can write these deadlines into your appointment book. You can provide yourself with daily "to do" lists that you write into your book. Even small, easy-to-do or habitual items could be added to the list. You can check the items off as you go along. The point is to register accomplishment tangibly as you move through the day. We all need to break a task down into manageable chunks which remove the threat of having to do a large task all at once. Sometimes, a task may be underestimated as costing very little energy and time when it really takes up a large chunk of your energies. Learn to break tasks down to 15 minute chunks to begin with. As you get more practiced at it, increase the size of your chunks. It would be very helpful to use your appointment book to plan your dechunking.

If you have read this far, you obviously have an interest in this topic, and you are likely wanting to achieve similar abundance, prosperity and growth in your own life as I have in mine. Below are Seven Principles of Prosperity that may be helpful in creating positive change in your life. I encourage you to try these techniques and see if they can help you to manifest your true heart's desires.

We need a pathway for the prosperity to enter our lives. The universe works in the same way. If you have a deep desire to do something specific with your life, you will be given the tools and resources to make it happen. Even if you can't imagine that possibility right now, be willing to suspend your disbelief. If you really do have blockages preventing you from creating what you want in life, you will find ways to hold yourself back from it if your dream makes you the least bit uncomfortable. For most of us, the thought of actually manifesting millions of dollars in our lives seems too impossible. If you are able to manifest a reasonable amount of abundance right now, you will gain confidence and be able to focus your efforts on greater abundance later.

The human mind is still a great mystery, especially the subconscious mind. Just like our outer circumstances can affect our health, so can our inner beliefs affect our physical reality. Take a few moments to think about things that may no longer be serving you, and ask yourself if you are willing to release them. This can be any number of things: stagnant relationships, too much idle time, or not enough discipline. We must affirm our intentions. From previous chapters you should have a clear idea of what you want and you know what you're willing to sacrifice. It's time to begin stating your intentions to the universe, in the form of affirmations. Affirmations are positive statements spoken, written or thought, though verbally seem to give stronger energy. Using the same example, you'd say, "I am a successful sculptor creating fulfilling and meaningful work. I work no more than 25 hours per week, and I earn $100,000.00 per year." You might also include some generic affirmations because they help reinforce what you're trying to accomplish. "I attract abundance and wealth. I deserve abundance and prosperity. I can achieve anything I desire." We must practice consistency of purpose. Many of us go wrong in being inconsistent. In order for affirmations and intentions to work, we need to keep working them. Say your affirmations as many times as you need to. Positive thinking is just like anything else, practice makes perfect. We can change whatever we choose, moment to moment.

We must have faith. If we don't believe we have what it takes, and if we don't believe we deserve to achieve our dreams, then we definitely won't. So in addition to changing your thoughts, be willing to take action! When your prosperity arrives, embrace it with joy, even if it arrives in a form you weren't expecting. Keep affirming aloud each day, "I accept the blessings the universe holds for me right now."

We must be patient with ourselves. Timing has a lot to do with the achievement of our dreams and goals. There are many factors we can't control, and timing is one of them. If we've reached the point where we've done all we can possibly do, then the wait can be maddening. But rather than sinking into frustration and despair, we can keep practicing active faith and affirmations, which lend positive energy to our vision. Keep infusing your energy into your dream to give it power to manifest.

Work on accepting your current circumstances. I know that's a tough pill to swallow if you are unhappy. But if you knew you were going to die tomorrow, would you have any regrets? What about those smaller, more precious moments in life? Would you regret not spending more time with your family, your friends, yourself? It seems that life has gotten so busy for most of us that we put them last. How do we find the time and energy to do what really matters? Most of us still have to work; we have responsibilities and demands on our time. The answer isn't so much about adding more to our lives, but rather, more deeply enjoying the lives we have now. Certainly we should follow our dreams and engage in fun activities. If you really want to sign up for those dance lessons, go for it. What transforms a person's life is how present they are in their day-to-day tasks. While you're at work, immerse yourself in the work. When you leave for the day, leave the work at work. Laugh, have fun, play. Engage meaningfully with your family. Let them know how much you love and appreciate them.

It is important to allow yourself to really experience life. We don't take time to awaken and enjoy. We are sleeping through the best parts of our lives. Live with passion, joy and awe. Cram as much happiness, fun and love into your life as you can. For those of us who spend much of our time helping and caring for others, it is too easy to neglect ourselves and become worn out, stressed out and run down.

Self-pampering is not about being selfish. It's about taking proper care of yourself and treating yourself as kindly as you treat others. We spend so much time and effort caring for our spouses, children, pets, friends, family members, employers and employees. Add to that volunteer activities, errands, housework, family functions, meetings, and there isn't much time left for caring for ourselves. Block the time out in your calendar and do not let anything interfere. As much as you do for others, you deserve the same time for yourself. You might have a hard time with this in the beginning. If your schedule is that full every day, then it is even more crucial to carve out some time for yourself. You may need to sacrifice something else to fit yourself in. Believe that you deserve to be cared for just as much as everyone else in your life does. In order to make time for yourself, you may need to say "no" to various extra obligations in your life. People will take advantage of us if we let them. I realized that it's as simple as saying, "I'm sorry, I'd love to help you out but I just can't right now."

Community is the sense of living and working together for common goals. We are naturally communal beings and derive great satisfaction from the experience of belonging to a group with a common purpose. Our society often fails to provide for this need, and unless we work to create community, it does not happen, or if it does so, it is sometimes in unhealthy ways. What makes family and community work is what you bring to it and the role you let it play in your life. This kind of connectedness gives us the power to improve our lives and make the world a better place.

Selfless service means giving of yourself to help others with no thought of return. Many religious traditions extol the ideal of selfless service as one of the great aids to dismantling the ego, cage and restructuring personality. Each day provides countless opportunities to practice putting others' interests ahead of your own, such as giving of your time, energy and presence to reduce the suffering or increase the happiness of others. The goal is not to acquire spiritual merit, increase your chances of going to heaven, or earn the admiration of the community. To love is to experience connection in its highest, purest form. We tend to confuse loving with other feelings that take us back into the world of separateness and fragmentation. Popular songs today seem to be mostly about the joys and pains of romantic love, not about loving as connection, which is something altogether different. Learning to love takes practice and time, especially in a culture that is focused so intensely on romantic love. In intimate relationships that work, the in-love state is replaced by mutual loving. That can happen only if both partners are mature and committed to a life together. Realizing that you have within you a limitless source of love that can benefit everyone and everything will help you form the best and strongest connections of your life.

Some cross-cultural research suggests that sexually repressed and touch-deprived societies are much more given to violence. Gain insight into issues such as aging, anxiety and depression, and learn more about overeating and mid-life concerns. I recommend incorporating some kind of service work into your weekly or monthly routine. Doing service work puts the needs of others ahead of your own, and that does good both for you and the people you're helping. It's easy to become overwhelmed by the amount of suffering in the world and all the people and causes in need of help. Think about your interests and pick an activity that you feel is most deserving of your time and energy.

If you have people in your life who have become dependent on you to do everything for them, you might face a bit more opposition. You may have a fight on your hands in order to make time for yourself. If you don't make the time to care for yourself, who else is going to? Look within your heart and see the bright, shining light of God there. Spend time working. Listen to soothing music or nature sounds. Treat yourself to lunch or dinner at a nice restaurant. Write your hopes, dreams and wishes in a journal. Watch a comedy or read something funny. Write a love letter to yourself and mail it. Take dance lessons. Learn a new language. Take pottery classes, or quilting classes, or learn how to make something for yourself. I am loved, and I love myself."

If you think of nature as a hostile force that is separate from yourself, you will go through life unnecessarily afraid and cut off from one of the great sources of spiritual nourishment. One way to connect with nature is through plants: gardening, collecting plants from the wild, growing cactuses and flowering bulbs. Having unusual and useful plants in and around the home can all help promote connectedness with nature. Plants can enrich your daily life, bring comfort and joy, and remind you that however you think of yourself, you are also part of the natural world.

If you wish to know the mind of a person, listen to their words. Are the words typically negative, critical, gossiping, deceptive, illusory, justifying, blaming, manipulative and argumentative? Are they uplifting, inspirational, positive, questioning, beautiful, loving, universal, truthful, accepting and supportive? We must use words carefully, remembering that words have a powerful long-lasting effect. As it goes, yesterday is a dream and tomorrow is a vision…but today, well lived, makes every yesterday a dream of happiness and every tomorrow a vision of hope. If you spend five minutes complaining, we have just wasted five minutes. We need to cast aside our doubts and make a total commitment to living the life we were meant to live.

We were not designed to be alone. Once you've mastered taking care of yourself, reach out to others. We need to feel whole and connected to loved ones and others. That will take effort, but it is rewarding work. We need to first focus on self and then reach out to others in positive ways. This helps us to feel whole and connected to others which take effort, but it is rewarding. Giving of yourself, spending time with friends and those in need to taking care of the environment or a companion animal also promotes positive interaction. We want and need the intimate support of a real family. Unfortunately, the nuclear family today is contracted. It is hard not to look at the "extended families" of some cultures with wistful longing, if not outright envy. Don't settle for nuclear family contraction, extend your network.

Self-assessment and Positive Self-talk

With so many things happening around us, it is important that we remember to embrace and love all of who you are past, present, and future. We need to forgive ourselves quickly and as often as necessary. We need to encourage ourselves. We need to tell ourselves good things about ourselves. We need to resist becoming a "spiritual sleeper." A spiritual sleeper lives in deep ignorance about themselves and the importance of their life. But if you asked them, they will insist that they are awake. It is easy to spot a spiritual sleeper. A sleeper reacts with anger, fearful emotions and haunting doubts.

There will always be a few misled people who may come into your life, drop by, phone to discourage you from having or following your dreams. They usually come with their thoughtless comments when you are in doubt and try to destroy your dreams. Hold on to your dreams! While it may be dark…morning comes and the sun will shine again.

We have heard the saying, if we keep doing what we have been doing, we will keep getting what we have been getting. Well if we continue to cling to the patterns we know inhibits our ability to discover what we don't know, we won't discover. It is easy to put off your dreams to sometimes in the future but based on what I have learned…"one of these days is none of these days."

History does not repeat itself, today is special and it will never return again. This day can make you believe that knowing really is doing. If you know but you don't act, then the results of your knowledge is like sense putting "none" (no action) in front of sense. You end up with "nonsense." This means to achieve anything, "doing" something is required. For many of us, because of fear of failure, there's a gap between knowing how to dream, achieve our dreams or goals and taking action, making the sacrifice by doing. Yet, once you close the gap and understand the universal truth of cause and effect, doing something in one area of your life will cause something to happen in other areas of your life. A special bond and unique relationship exists between knowing and doing. We need to keep that affirmation alive by learning how to harness our creative genius, stimulating our intellectual abilities, and attaining blissful calm, the serenity of true inner peace. Affirmations help us to make a difference in the world and enhance both our personal and professional development and evolution. They will help bring us to new heights catapulting us into a higher level of consciousness and a wider spectrum of inner harmony and peace. Encourage yourself. Tell yourself good things about yourself!

Principles

- Every action is preceded by a thought, to heal the pain of our past, we must change the way we think, so our actions and behaviors also change.

- Focus on the experiences and patterns in your life that gave you a feeling of happiness, hope and healing.

7
LETTING GO OF CLUTTER IN YOUR MIND

"Hold fast to dreams, for if dreams die, life is a broken winged bird that cannot fly."

— Langston Hughes, *Dreams from Collected Poems*

Positive Thinking Makes Good Memories

One of the consequences of negative thinking is failing to see the bright side of life and the creation of unpleasant memories. We often hear people reminiscing about the good old days and how good they were. Our emotional intelligence or emotional health is our ability to attend quickly, appropriately and without effort to our reminiscing about memories and feelings which leads to the most favorable response. Emotional incompetence which I call ill health occurs when we are not able to attend rapidly, appropriately and effortlessly to our feelings causing self-damaging emotions and behaviors.

All of us have fond memories of things that went well, memories of times we loved and memories of beauty we have seen or felt. Memories allow us to feel joy in the midst of sorrow. Memories allow us to smell a rose, even when the snow is two feet deep. How we spend our days is, of course, how we spend our lives. When we spend so much time in our memories, we lose the power of the moment because we are so rarely in it; we are living in the past. Our memories help us to focus on reliving the past or speculating about the future. If we can treasure each moment, our lives will be rich, no matter what we have accomplished. No reward is offered for our past, it is gone forever. If, before going to bed every night, we tear a page from the calendar, and make a note, there goes another day of my life, never to return, we will become more time conscious. Awareness is the key to all change. Develop a higher awareness, in order to find your authentic self and open the door to new possibilities by using your imagination and intuition. Positive thoughts are not the denial bad experiences in your life, it's just another way of seeing things, alternate perception that puts negative things in perspective. Live long and live well.

Letting the Past Go

Forgiveness and letting go can help you manage anger, cut stress and improve health. But most important, letting go can help you get out of the prison your lack of forgiving has created for you. Our minds mold our experiences. It holds onto everything we experience. When anxiety and nervous tension become chronic, our body and mind gradually wear down into a state of weakness and ill-health. The energy flow of the body, concentration, and clarity of the mind are disturbed. Our organs begin to malfunction. At some point, a psychosomatic illness is created. Negative emotions such as bitterness, fear, anger, hate, envy, jealousy and resentment may begin to dominate our mind. When this happens, our relationships with loved ones begin to deteriorate and a feeling of alienation and isolation may set in. At that point, it is time for a mind makeover, what some call an "attitude adjustment." An attitude adjustment means to change negative, life-destroying feelings into positive life-building attitudes.

The key is developing the ability to forgive. Forgiving is not so important for helping the others as it is for helping ourselves. We actually gain much more when we forgive others for a real or perceived transgression. When we hold negative feelings towards others, we block the free flow of natural life supporting energies in our own bodies. Those negative feelings suppress our happiness. Being unable to forgive and holding onto negative feelings tenses our nervous system, not the other person's. It inhibits our adrenal glands and immunological system. Everyday, it seems, we hear about someone who is suffering from negative feelings toward people (living or dead). While we may have reasons to feel hurt, rejection, anger, injustice, hate and revenge, they will destroy our health, happiness, and our internal and external harmony. The person we are unable to forgive is not nearly as affected. For example, many of us know people who have been holding on to anger and hate towards their parents, another family member or a loved one for decades. These feelings have been undermining both their physical and emotional well-being. They are not only suffering from their feelings but also from guilt about those feelings, compounding the problem.

Remember, life has given us at every moment exactly what we need for the next step on our growth process. We have the power...it may not be easy but imagine being free of worry, anxiety, envy, fear, anger and despair. Let past opinions go. Just smile...take a deep, deep breath...let the worries of the day go!

Instead of being angry about the past or anxious about the future, we can let go. Your ego and reflections of the past have only the power that you give them. You can choose at any time to free yourself from the limitations they impose on you. Life's dreams are more than just places to go, people to know, things to acquire, and experiences to have. Our dreams express who we are. Behind every dream is a purpose. That purpose is, and always has been, ours to command. People stay in dead-end careers, loveless marriages and never leave the borders of their hometowns. People are willing to live a mediocre life for the security they think it provides. But what if you were guaranteed a positive outcome? How would you live your life differently? Every day we make choices. If we want to lose weight, we must stop eating fatty foods. Making choices today may seem hard but tomorrow offers new opportunities. Each step creates a new road map with the possibility of transforming our past. Our loss today will afford us with the opportunity for new choices. We can mourn the past and celebrate the future. While we know that people have a hard time letting go of bad habits, resentments and their suffering, we must chose to live our life much better then we are living. We can honor our experiences to date, that which brought us to this point and still create a new future. So let go, begin to celebrate your new beginning and allow yourselves to venture past your ego. We'll find the new freedom achieving our dreams and success to be exciting. Live all the days of your life. Be healthy and be happy.

Embracing Hard Times and Enhancing Achievement

Instinctively, we know that anyone who has done something worthwhile has overcome hard times. Our success in life depends upon us being resilient, with clear goals and indomitable spirits. We grow that way. Most of us spend our lives trying to avoid hard times. While we shouldn't seek hard times, when they come, we should welcome the challenge as a worthy foe; we should realize that through our interaction with hard times, we become a better person. Every contact we have with difficulty gives us the opportunity to grow personally and professionally and to forge a character that will enable us to achieve much later on.

With that in mind, here are some thoughts on hard times. Hard times can help us to succeed in every area of our life and achieve our dreams. Hard times bring out our resources. As my mother once said, "Hard times are like the seasons, fall and winter but if we hold on spring and summer are sure to come and the same can be said for life." When everything is going well, we coast. Hard times, keeps us sharp. It keeps us using our attributes and strengths. Hard times can make enemies friend. As a former basketball player, despite any difference we may have had off the court, we worked as a team on the hardwood. These should remind us that the next time we experience challenges, consider how they can be used to bring us closer to our friends, family, our network or our team. We should not underestimate hard times, they serve to help make us better people with stronger characters. Courage, discipline and perseverance will never flourish unless they are. Without hard times, without variety, life is boring. Hard times make life interesting. If we are in the middle of some difficulty right now, what resources are we drawing on? Who are we drawing closer to and working with? Every hard time, every failure, every heartache carries with it the seed of an equal or greater benefit.

Everything that happens in our outside world begins in our inside world. Our actions start out as thoughts, either conscious or subconscious. We should take some time today to read a book or listen to some material that will change us on the inside. Our optimism or pessimism is the way we interpret the past, the way we experience and view the present and the way we imagine the future. Have you given much thought about how your attitude, whether you are an optimist or a pessimist, affects you professionally? Have you thought about how it affects you personally? Optimism breathes life into you each day. Pessimism drains you. Optimism helps you to take needed risks. Pessimism plays it safe and never accomplishes much. Optimism improves those around you. Pessimism drags you down. Optimism inspires people to great heights. Pessimism deflates people to new lows. If you are an optimist, you will generally find that good things happen to you. I choose to be an optimist. If things go awry, at least I have spent my time beforehand enjoying life and not worrying about it. And, being an optimist, I view the "negative" situation as an opportunity to grow and learn. Become an optimist and see your world change before your eyes.

Clean Up Clutter

As the seasons change often, we hear people say, it is about time to clean out the closets. We throw away things we no longer wear or need. We clean things we don't generally clean. Where we live represents who we are and our house symbolically represents our emotional state, our dreams, feeling and purpose in life. Clutter takes over our kitchen counters, bedside, household desks, office credenzas, book bags, binders and lockers. Don't forget the closets and the attics, the garage and the basement. I have a dream. My dream is that I will simply run my hand across my desk and the piles, messages, files and to-do lists will disappear. I have a dream that I will close my eyes and every photo gets put in an album, every letter is answered promptly, every surface, box and pile is gone, done. It's a great dream.

We are a generation that was supposed to be electronic and paper-free, but we certainly have amassed a lot of stuff. Clutter invades our lives and stare us in the face. Will there ever be enough time to sort it through? Instead of the physical cleaning, see today as the beginning of a new day, the day that we focus time on ourselves, to do a spiritual and psychological cleaning. Instead of crumbs in drawers, we have a chance to cast our crumbs on the water of knowledge and understanding. And with each crumb, we let go of our past failings, criticism and heartache. Instead of cleaning the pantry and the fridge, inside and out, we cleanse our souls. Instead of realigning cupboards, we reassess relationships with family and friends. Instead of putting our house in order literally, we gather our family and friends for a reunion and try to put our house in order spiritually. Instead of e-mails and junk mail, let's write cards and letters with positive thoughts and loving messages as the vehicle to send love and forgiveness.

It may be therapeutic to do reflective thinking and take time to smell the flowers and eat sweet apples and honey. It is a sensory experience that awakens our souls. But so often the clutter of our lives gets in the way. We should be thankful for life and health, but it is often more difficult than we thought, because hearts and minds are cluttered with hurt feelings, problems and headaches, disappointments and injustice, heartache and grief. Our lives are cluttered beyond belief with wounds that have never healed, because we refused to address them or make them better. How many rooms in homes have been closed off to family or friends because there is too much clutter for anyone to be comfortable? If our physical lives get so easily cluttered, what about our psychological, emotional and spiritual lives? Is it cluttered? Our inner self never seems to be as urgent as the deadlines imposed on us from outside by work, school, family, store hours, things that break in the house just when you have no time to fix them, etc.

But our inner self is more important than all those outside influences, and it needs a spring cleaning as much as our closets, bedrooms, living room, kitchens, basements, laundry room or our cars. We should do ourselves a favor. We should take the next few weeks to dump all the trash and clutter we have held for too long. Let go of all that takes up too much space in your heart and mind, and just throw it away. This is my hope in every message that I pray, that with every song we sing, and each message we read will call us to make life more livable. We can't take a vacation from ourselves...it is our duty to be ourselves, to be our best selves and make a difference in the world.

I wish I could wave my hand over your hearts to lift all the emotional and psychological clutter you have buried deep inside. I close my eyes and the beginning of a new day restores your troubled soul. I run my hand across your calendar to make spiritual space and healing, to make time for rest and study. I may not be able to do all of that, but you can. As the new season approaches, we need to find our way to achieving happiness with thought, purpose and peace.

Principles

- Happiness does not lie at the bottom of the glass or in a shopping mall, we must let go and move on remembering that happiness can not be bought, it can be achieved.
- Belief in the way that our life should be, stops us from enjoying what we have and what could be.

8
ROAD MAP TO SUCCESS

"To be a poor man is hard, but to be a poor race in a land of dollars is the very bottom of hardship."

— W. E. B. DuBois, *The Souls of Black Folk*

Plan to Succeed or Fail to Plan

The way we think becomes continual and repetitive, over time, it will affect our beliefs, decisions and actions. However, like any bad habit, we can change negative thought patterns once we are aware of them. If we try are objective, we can identify the real reason for the way we think and find an alternative point of view. We can decide to focus on something positive to replace the negative mindset. For instance, after an argument with a friend, we may be filled with hatred and experience a range of negative emotions, which ensure you take no constructive action. On the other hand, if we respond in a positive way which acknowledges that we can learn something valuable from considering another point of view, it will be much easier to compromise and move forward.

Some of us seem to be born pessimists. Perhaps this is because certain people with inquisitive minds also see the possible pitfalls and limitations that come with new ideas and opportunities. If you are like that, there is still a way to use pessimism constructively. Imagining even the worst scenario can help you plan strategies to ensure success. Even if you cannot forget there is a chance of failure, do not let things rest there. Instead, ask yourself what could possibly go wrong and then plan appropriate action to minimize the risks.

Even the most positive people will sometimes feel anxious, particularly when facing new challenges or difficult circumstances. But our fear should not stop us from pursuing our goals. We accept the fear, focus on the tasks and activities that will lead to success and move forward towards our dreams. Research from the emerging field of positive psychology has shown another way to feel empowered. By focusing on strengths and enhancing them, rather than trying to compensate for our weaknesses, we significantly increase our chances of success. By approaching problems and challenges this way, we will be ready to seize the big opportunity when it comes.

Unconsciously, we attract everything. That's why we have to read the books, like *Dream Greatness Be Unstoppable* so that we can begin to wake up. We can begin to take conscious control of what we've been doing unconsciously. At this point, we can plan to succeed by looking at why did we attract our situation or circumstance? We can't get what we want in life until we know what we want in life. We will either plan to succeed or by not planning, plan to fail. We all have thoughts, some are positive and some are negative. With our personal plan, we begin to notice which ones are the ones that make us feel good and we want to reach for the thoughts that feel good. We begin to go in the direction of having more of feel good positive thoughts. Our experience teaches us that we get more of whatever we focus on. As we focus on positive thoughts, our negative thoughts will decrease or we just won't pay much attention to them.

We may complain that we do not have enough time or we just don't get enough done. Do you sometimes feel like you do not have enough time to get it all done? Here's a way to redeem the time. One of the problems with planning is that most people feel they must decide now when each task will be done, which creates unhealthy pressure. The way around this problem is to create a master list of everything that needs to be done, and then use your master list to plan. When a new task needs to be added to a list, add it to this list. Having a master list, only one list provides peace of mind since we don't have to worry about forgetting those important things that need our attention. In order to have a plan, we have to set aside quiet time to plan.

There are a series of expected life stages that we all go through in our journey through life. Some people give names to the stages such as hesitant and uncertain; transitions, dedicated, mid-life and leaving a heritage. At each stage we tend to reassess and re-balance our life values priorities. It's helpful to know where we are so that when we pass through a stage we can be aware of what's happening and where we want to go from there. This book puts you back into the driver's seat of your life and provides you with the road map you need to get to the life of your dreams.

Dreams are the keys to your ultimate destination in life, while goals are the intermediate steps along the way. *Dreams* represent what you want and why, while *goals* represent your plan of action that will get you there. *Goals and dreams* complement one another. *Wishes* are things that you potentially desire or want without having to commit to any physical act. When you have a wish that you really want to accomplish, you simply convert it into a dream or into a goal towards which effort is directed.

The difference between *dreams and goals* is somewhat subtle. A dream is a type of target. The first type of target is what is commonly called a SMART goal. SMART acronym: (S— Savvy M— Measurable A— Active R—Reachable T—Timed) goals which translates to: S—Savvy goals are those that grow out of our dreams. They are goals we can sink your teeth into; goals that get us excited. M—Measurable goals clearly define what it is we're going to do. A—Active goals say exactly what action we're going to take. R—Reachable goals should challenge or stretch us, but they should also be reachable. Reachable goals also take into account our own abilities. T—Timed goals are timed goals, goals with deadlines—a specific date or some other unit of time by which the goal will be achieved. The best SMART goals are focused, specific, short-term targets that involve things that are under your direct control. If you only use SMART goals, you run the risk of losing sight of the big picture, the reasons why you are setting goals in the first place. SMART goals can help you climb the ladder of success step-by-step, oftentimes to find that your ladder is leaning against the wrong wall.

A *dream* is the ultimate realization of your desire or wish, and it is not limited by the SMART constraints. Dreams are your ultimate destination or target; someone or something at which you have taken aim: an area, surface, object, or person. For example, the bird's bright plumage makes it an easy target. If you only have dreams and no goals to support them, you can easily feel overwhelmed by the enormity of your dream. The shorter-term goals provide achievable intermediate targets that serve as stepping stones toward your ultimate dream. If you have goals but no dreams, you can easily fall into the trap of focusing so much on the steps that you lose sight of your destination.

Dreams also help you evaluate whether your overall strategy and associated goals are working or not. Without the dream, you can pursue goal after goal and not really make any progress. In general, goals require more detail than dreams, but they are also more short-lived because they represent specific and focused targets. Goals are much more specific and focused than the dream which may have inspired them. However, having the dream allows you to keep sight of the big picture and periodically evaluate the goals to determine if they are still helping you move towards your dream.

Achieving your dreams and goals depends on several factors: 1) having a specific goal, 2) certainty, that you really want to achieve your goal, 3) a clear mental image of your goal, 4) the will to disregard and reject doubts and thoughts about failure, 5) confidence and faith and persevere until you gain success.

By thinking in a positive manner about your goal, and not allowing any doubts to enter your mind, your intuition starts working, you see opportunities, and you have energy at your disposal to follow your goals and dreams. You actively develop your inner powers.

This should not be a tough ordeal. Success does not require hard physical labor. In fact, you need mental work. You need to dream and affirm your dreams in your mind. Dreaming and affirmation are an important part of achieving success. When you dream and affirm, you focus and channel your energies toward your goal. Your mind is geared toward finding solutions to bring your dreams and goal to fruition.

Many people only focus on extremely large goals, such as becoming wealthy, getting an expensive car, possessing a big house or building a very successful business. But small daily goals such as getting to work on time, spending more time with the family or loved ones, reading a book, going to see a movie and eating less for your health are important steps in achieving your big dreams and goals.

As it is with any plan, we need priorities. A task is not an "A" task unless it costs you money, or will ruin your reputation if you fail to do it. "B" tasks are important, but the world will not end if you don't do them. Everything else is a "C" task. Using this method will cause you to list fewer "A" tasks but likely get more of them done. Treat it like any other appointment. Monthly planning is too long range and daily planning can dissolve into simply managing the next crisis. Remember, you are in control. Start by placing "A" tasks down as if they were appointments, because now they are. "B" tasks can be handled when you have open time while "C" tasks may simply have to wait. Being immovable is the key. You have planned your week, and unless it's very serious, don't change your plan.

As the saying goes, "Failure to plan means planning to fail." In today's fast changing world, change and unpredictability have become the norm. Flexible planning makes excellent sense if you hope to obtain and maintain a stable source of income and a satisfying work life. Set a deadline for your goal. Then, work backward to create a to-do list each week. If you wanted to send your mailing out on September 1, you would write, "edit mailing" on August 30, and "finish creating mailing" on August 29 and so on. We need to spend time each day planning. Take 15 minutes every day to create a plan. If you follow the example above, you'll have a broad plan to follow. You'll need to spend some time planning to include unexpected things into your day. We need to develop a to-do list. Keep your priorities on your to-do list. Put incidentals or non-essential tasks on sticky notes. Planning to succeed doesn't have to be intimidating or overwhelming. Failing to plan is planning to fail. Planning and time management is basically a matter of setting goals for where you want to go and what you want to do, and then developing a plan for reaching those goals. It is important to think in terms of "making" or "taking" time rather than finding time. To redeem time means to convert it into something of value. Here's a way to redeem the time. We all know, the key to time management is to plan to ensure important tasks are done. One of the problems with planning is that most people feel they must decide now when each task will be done, which creates unhealthy pressure. When a new task needs to be added to a list, add it to this list. To have a plan, set aside quite time, calm your mind, focus and let the details flow.

You may have heard the story of a top insurance agent on the West Coast. The president of a company wanted to see him on a particular Tuesday, but didn't call until Monday. Firmly and politely the agent told the president that he couldn't see him until Friday. When they saw each other on Friday, the president inquired where he had been all week. "Right here in L.A." the agent replied. More than a little steamed, the president said, "I had to take two out-of-the-way flights to re-arrange for Friday." The agent's reply was straight to the point. "I spent four hours planning my week before you called me." He showed the president what he had done on Tuesday. It was impressive to say the least. Then he made this simple statement. "Mr. President, the reason I'm your #1 agent is that I don't allow anyone or anything to disrupt the time I set aside for each client." With this he couldn't argue.

When you learn to do things in their order of importance, the feeling of "There's something I'm supposed to do, but what is it?" will leave you entirely. This frees your mind. Keep yourself on track by asking, "What is the best use of my time for the next 30 minutes?" Plan your life work and you will succeed.

Discover the Secrets for Creating Success

Self-esteem increases your confidence and is the key to bringing more fulfillments to your life. You can create the life you want with a little practice. You can enjoy life while you accomplish all your goals. You can teach yourself and develop simple system to master your inner powers, increase your self-confidence and enjoy success after success in only a few minutes of your day. Develop a plan to eliminate stress; take control of your life; create fulfilling relationships; be more confident in social situations; meet new people; improve your finances; boost your creativity; increase self esteem and self confidence; stop worrying; enjoy inner peace; succeed in business; enjoy better health; meet the perfect partner; eliminate negative feelings; take charge of your life; get a better job and create and alter situations to what you want.

Some people refer to your hidden abilities as mind power, while a number of people will tell you it's the power of the subconscious mind, or the power of positive thinking. In order to create the change you want we need to start by sending the right messages to your subconscious mind. We have untapped power within our mind. We were all born with these powers, but we have never learned how to master them. If you believe, you can learn to master this amazing gift by understanding the power of your mind.

Scientists have proven that we only use ten percent of our mind. The rest is never used effectively. Imagine what would happen if we used our mind to its fullest. We would stop getting sick and live healthier, more productive lives. Researchers have proven that people who incorporate positive thinking live better lives. Why? Because, they know how to use the power of their mind. Unfortunately, most people never get their mind working for them. Instead, they let their mind, work against them, creating things they don't want. The mind and subconscious mind create everything in life. We must learn how to get them working for us so we can create what we want in life. Develop your intuition by tapping into the power of your subconscious mind.

Throughout life, we have been taught all kinds of things about creating change. If we really want to create change we must nurture and develop our subconscious mind. Developing the subconscious mind is much like raising a child. Your subconscious mind creates everything in your life based on the messages and information you send to it. You are constantly sending messages and information to your subconscious mind and many of those messages are useless or are working against you. Your messages to your subconscious mind are your thoughts, beliefs and actions. So if you constantly worry about not having enough money you will never have enough money. If you don't think you're capable of accomplishing your goals you will never accomplish any of them. If you don't think there are enough opportunities for you, you will never find the right opportunity. If you think you're overweight, you will always be overweight. Because your subconscious mind is always working on the information you send it and if that information is negative then you will only have a negative reality. Once your subconscious mind gets your message it then connects with the people and events that will help create the situation based on your message. It's important to understand that your messages to your subconscious mind are not just your thoughts! To create the changes you want, you need to create a new way of living.

Books on positive thinking promise to change your life. But by the time you're finished reading it you've forgotten most of the information. In order to change your life, you need to take control of your mind right now and no book, software, CD or tape alone is going to do the trick. We don't need to spend a fortune on a personal coach, books, useless CD's, tapes and software. Using our mind and subconscious mind, we have the keys in our own hands. We can have it all, today. We can master our own powers and turn to them whenever we want for the rest of Developing the subconscious mind is much like raising a child. Your subconscious mind creates everything in your life based on the messages and information you send to it. You are constantly sending messages and information to your subconscious mind and many of those messages are useless or are working against you. Your messages to your subconscious mind are your thoughts, beliefs and actions. So if you constantly worry about not having enough money you'll never have enough money. If you don't think you're capable of accomplishing your goals you'll never accomplish any of them. If you don't think there are enough opportunities for you, you'll never find the right opportunity. If you think you're overweight, you'll always be overweight. Because your subconscious mind is always working on the information you send it and if that information is negative then you will only have a negative reality. Once your subconscious mind gets your message it then connects with the people and events that will help create the situation based on your message. It's important to understand that your messages to your subconscious mind are not just your thoughts. To create the changes you want, you need to create a new way of living.

Dreaming Big to Overcome Circumstances

People with big dreams and with a positive outlook on life achieve better grades in high school and generally outperform pessimists in the workplace. Optimism is also a recurring theme in the most inspiring success stories of our time. Oprah Winfrey, known as the most influential woman in America, began her career as a humble radio reporter in Nashville. Her passion allowed her to overcome sexism, racism and a host of personal challenges to become the queen of daytime television. Similarly, Richard Branson, founder and chairman of the London-based Virgin Group, struggled with dyslexia and disappointing exam results at school. Even so, he set up a hugely successful student paper, making use of his now-famous energy and entrepreneurial spirit, and went on to build a business empire. Neither could have made it to such heights without a dream and positive thinking. Dreaming is a gift we all have and we can develop the same attitude.

I am a believer in visualization and the power of positive thinking. The power of the mind can help you to fight cancer, recover from surgery and overcome problems. It is not as simple as waking up one morning and deciding you're going to see the positive in everything, there are a number of strategies such as Neuro Linguistic Programming (NLP) to help you make the most of your mind power. In thinking, you use all the senses, not just your eyes to dream or imagine what the situation will be like. You also factor in the possibilities of what could happen on the day and how you would like to react.

Some people focus only on the immediate and the specific, never putting efforts into perspective. It's a matter of style. Risk involves developing the ability to be a change agent. If you expect change then you must be willing to change. Dreaming implies taking risks and doing something to make our communities a better place to live. Leaders are always flying blind. You can't make uncertainty disappear but you can isolate it. Success and risk travel the same road. On your journey to success, you will find risks. We want to be successful by clarifying uncertainties and reduce risks that endanger success. Risk is a given. We need to understand risk and begin to make sense of uncertainty. We need to isolate the elements of uncertainty and evaluate them one at a time. Begin by answering four basic questions:

- What are the key uncertainties?
- What are the possible outcomes of these uncertainties?
- What are the chances that each possible outcome will occur?
- What are the consequences of each outcome?

Next, construct a risk profile. Third, clarify the uncertainties, outcomes, chances, and consequences that will affect your decision. Which of the key uncertainties will most impact the success or failure of your objective? Some uncertainties have a small number of outcomes. Others will have a large number of potential outcomes. Judge the chances that each outcome will occur. Since different outcomes will have different consequences, you should make an informed choice. Use your personal experience; gather existing information; conduct research; collect new data; through surveys; and consult experts. When expressing chances, avoid vague terms like "fairly likely" or "a good chance." Clarify the consequences of each outcome.

Making a decision in the face of uncertainty requires that we choose among risks. By developing a risk profile, you can eliminate the chance of poor choices. The best option will be obvious. If you still find it hard to make a decision or make up your mind, you need to focus on your risk tolerance. If, you are risk averse, the downside will weigh more heavily in your mind than the upside. The more deeply we fear the outcome, the more risk averse we are. Flawed thinking leads to flawed life decisions. We represent the best but maybe we're still not sure about what we want to do, our goals or personal/professional plans. Uncertainty doesn't have to mean fear; it can mean possibility. Striking out never stop a home run hitter from swinging at bat. Seek and seize opportunities. If we fail, we get up…two; three, and four times we get up. Never let the fear of failure get in our way. Shoot for the moon and land on the stars, just keep trying. This is our day and we deserve this day. We deserve only the best. We all have warm weather friends who may not encourage us to succeed or to be our best; don't let negative talk stop you. Do your best to outlast all the negative talkers. Hang in there don't be confined by other people's definitions of good or best. See to be and the best person possible we will become.Focusing on self-awareness and control are critical success tools. The following strategies have been identified in managing the stresses associated with the new workgroup relationships.

- Assess your personality strengths and limitations.

- Recognize and assess your communication style. This includes both oral and non-verbal communication. Some people talk on and on and use big words because they think it makes them sound important.

- Develop our ability to maintain composure under fire. If we don't prepare, we'll get burned. We need to develop the ability to turn difficult situations into positive situations by identifying and developing strategies which will help to minimize or eliminate the problem.

- Build on past struggles and successes. Lessons learned from history teach us that we have the ability and power to overcome extreme circumstances. Trust and understanding strengthen relationships. Getting to know another personality is a slow process. The larger the group, the longer it takes. No one trusts a stranger, yet we demand trust. We must create new opportunities to get to know and understand other personality styles. Personality styles are developed over time and experienced and evidenced by how we react to events and other people. Psychologist colors, animals, sensory perceptions, and so forth to define styles. There are many other styles too numerous to define. The style is in the eye of the beholders. We tend to adopt the styles of our parents or the opposite styles of our parents if we reject their teaching. If we looked at the personality style of our supervisor or the leader of our group we may identify that person as an angry bull as a fearful chicken spinning out of control, or inferior. Since most of us accept the notion that people are who they are and, therefore, we should not try to change another person. But we can work with other styles and help create interpersonal change. Create opportunities to develop relationships and have fun with other personalities. If we are to succeed we must understand that business is not more important than our relationships.

Change involves conflict and we need to create skills to handle conflict. When we think of task oriented styles, we think of people who get pleasure from getting results. The process-oriented style might get pleasure from working with people. The task and process oriented styles see things from different perspectives. Neither task nor process oriented style is right or wrong. It's just a difference in orientation. All styles are needed. If we are to succeed individually or as a group, it is important that each style understands the needs of the others.

Words that Speak Success

Words hold power beyond their meanings. A term used in one context or by a certain group may constitute another perspective in another context or to someone else. Word meanings change and evolve, often cannot be fully described in a few sentences. When you speak, your words are more important to your overall "believability" than you would think. During one of my recent presentations, I woke up the audience by suddenly stepping out from behind the podium and throwing my prepared speech into the air with a hearty laugh. My actions immediately implanted the idea I was presenting; words delivered with passion and not words delivered as if read from a sheet of paper. The words that you speak are important and key part of communication. The "three V's" of spoken communication include: verbal, the words that you speak...almost as if they were peeled right off the page; vocal, the way that you say those words...intonation and projection; and visual, the way you look and act while you are speaking. Most speakers concentrate on the verbal element, treating the words as if they are the communication. "Believability" is used to describe how much we are in harmony with all three elements of communication. In short, doing great science doesn't earn you much if you can't talk about it in a way that will win over your audience.

Remember to count five seconds for eye contact with audience members. It takes that long to transfer your enthusiasm and passion through your eyes. Your gestures and smile, how your eyes connect with your audience ... these issues and more are what determine greater than fifty percent of our believability. Your audience will use your eye contact and energy to determine your Likability. Developing good communication skills is critical for success, but it can be a lifelong pursuit.

Words are our most effective means of advertising who we are and what we are all about. Potential professional or personal relationships are often won over by the first impression made by the words we use. Each time that we speak to a group, our message can extend exponentially as your listeners talk to their friends, family and coworkers. Unfortunately, too many of us take speaking and words for granted. Words effectively represent who we are to the outside world and allows for us to transmit our perceptions. Words provide clarity for our thoughts. Successful people use techniques called power words when used effectively are like hypnosis to the hearers. For example, we use gestures as we talk to help make our point. Those movements correspond to the sound patterns patterned on the individual words. Under emotional stress, words prescribe action.

Words are a valuable tool when it comes to getting along with other people and getting what you want from life. Words are the most obvious thing in the world and may be the most overlooked. The world's most successful, highest-earning people typically possess a rich, well-developed vocabulary and superior communication skills not just average, but superior. Every day, people judge us by the words we choose. Whether what they think is true or not, what you say says a lot about your intelligence, education, and status.

Generally, when people get their own way with others, they do it with words. They want others to agree with their point of view, give them what they want, do what they ask and buy what they are selling. From the car salesman's hard sell, the hammering of TV commercials, the relative's request for a loan, the doctor's diagnosis to the child's pleading to stay up late, the seduction and/or assault of words is continuous. Whether professional or personal relationships between one person's desires and another's, some people find they always lose, are convinced they must be wrong, while others consistently win; their logic, their reasons are so powerful, so compelling, they almost force others to change their opinions, their beliefs and their behavior to comply with what's being asked. This enormous power is in the meaning of the words, what they mean to the person respond to them.

Nothing makes a stronger and more lasting impression than a strong command of the English language. And conversely, nothing can hinder the achievement of your career goals and the recognition you truly deserve more than your lack of it. Language and communication are at the heart of our professional and personal experiences, whether communication takes place face-to-face, or in writing. People must have the linguistic and cultural skills to communicate successfully in a pluralistic society.

It's strange and unfortunate but the great majority of adults have an eighth or ninth grade vocabulary. They cripple themselves in the most vital aspect of successful living. Words are tools which express our thoughts and desires to others and the more tools we have in the toolbox, the more jobs we can handle. The way we use language typically provides a clue to one's education level. In the old days, people used to "bad mouth" what they called "book learning." This idea was reminiscence of the dark ages when people were suspicious of anything they didn't understand. I remember, as a kid, hearing complaints about people spending too much time in school instead of getting a job, the way the complainer had to do.

All knowledge is acquired through reading, listening, observing, and practicing. The more we engage in these activities, the more knowledge we acquire. Knowledge still is power to the person who has it and the use of language, more than any other thing, is a barometer of a person's knowledge. According to research on university students' vocabulary skills at graduation, after five years, ten, and fifteen years, the results showed, without a single exception, those students who scored highest in vocabulary were doing best in their careers. They had better jobs and were making more money.

Anyone can have an excellent vocabulary, but very few do. There are several wonderful language and vocabulary books and programs in every bookstore or library. But it means work, so many people choose to slip along using eighth grade vocabulary and then wonder why they do not progress in their careers.

A funny aspect of our society is the number of people who poke fun at those who speak with a foreign accent. Whenever you hear a foreign accent, it means the person can speak at least two languages. Those who laugh, as a rule, cannot even speak their own language very well. A simple way to improve your vocabulary is to get resources you need on the language you wish to learn including a good dictionary. Make sure you know the pronunciation key and what the symbols mean in your dictionary. Study the language an hour a day, each day. Whenever you come across a word you are not sure of, look it up, and then write it down in your vocabulary book along with its meaning. Usually, this will help you remember it. Start working your new words into your vocabulary where you are sure they fit.

Pay close attention in meetings, during seminars and conferences, or simply in conversation, and listen for new words or words you don't fully understand. Most of us don't use vocabulary as a litmus test when making friends, but we should spend time with well-spoken people. If we find ourselves in the company of somebody who speaks well, it's a great learning experience to converse with them. We should seek out people who have mastered of expressing themselves. When you spend time with these people, their good habits can rub off on you; eloquence can rub off.

An effective process for internalizing new words is to repeat saying a word out loud and defining the word out loud numerous times. Then, find a sentence using that word and say that sentence aloud the same number of times. The repetition will help assimilate that word into your active vocabulary. Expanding your vocabulary is a matter of repetition and persistence. Habitual vocabulary is so ingrained in speech patterns that it's hard to modify, but if you continue to work at it diligently, a more expansive and stronger vocabulary will emerge.

Your vocabulary is how you express yourself and your ideas. If you're using the right words to express your ideas and beliefs, you're going to look sharp. A good vocabulary is going to denote that you may be more educated and sharper than a competitor for the same personal or professional position. The trick isn't using a rare, esoteric five-syllable term that only one percent of the population would ever understand. Rather, it is using "power words," words that send a strong message and convey your powerful grasp of the language without leaving your audience in the dark. If you set aside one-hour a day, six days a week, it would come to 312 hours a year. It would not take long to become an expert at just about anything using this strategy.

Let us endeavor to listen to the word of wisdom and to learn to use our words with care. We need to identify the awesome power behind the spoken word, and how begin to use it to maximum effect, to create the world we so much deserve.

Surviving in a Hostile Environment

As a leader, you must possess the skills to build your teams around the right personalities and to manage those personalities. We all see the world from our own unique perspective, our own paradigm. When you're part of a team, you bring that paradigm to the team environment. Personality traits within a team can offset one another and build on each other and lead to synergies. Rather than ask each team member to conform to a group norm, you must recognize and utilize personality differences to ensure high performance. One way to spot and manage certain personality traits and inhibitors is through emotional intelligence and mental skills, emphasizing the mind where battles are truly won and lost.

You must have mental skills beyond technical competence. You need to expand your circle of influence by never letting the enemy into your mind. You need to maintain the ability to choose, project a positive attitude and defining goals increasing the probability of long-term success n stressful environments. Managing conflict in the workplace is a time-consuming but necessary task. The conflicts may range from disagreements to major controversies that may lead to litigation or violence. Conflicts have an adverse effect on productivity and morale. They may result in high employee turnover and certainly limit staff contributions and impede efficiency.

Put on the armor of faith, purpose and remember those who sacrificed for your well being. Getting through the hostile environment is preparing you for what faith, belief and those who sacrificed for you had in mind for you. The level of your faith is determined by how you handle any situation. Your rewards come from your faith, belief and from acknowledging those who sacrificed for you. Stop trying to get folks to validate what you do. Don't come to work to have personal relationships. Remember, what got you to where you are your, faith, belief, and those who sacrificed for you.

We can change our atmosphere without commenting on the problem. We have to seek opportunities to change the atmosphere without commenting on the problems. Stop allowing your mouth to spread negativity. Complaining is negative and nobody wants to be around negative people. Complaining is a symbol of failure.

Do your job well, but remember your mission. When you do your job well, you're modeling. We need more models for good performance. We need your smile, your positive attitude, the optimism that is inside of you. We're supposed to be influencing our environments, not the environment influencing us. Stop going to work to receive; go to work to give. Stop hanging around negative people. These people carry the spirit of confusion, and ungratefulness. Remember, when there's a crack in the foundation of a boat, water gets in and eventually the boat sinks. Don't allow the atmosphere and folk's negativity and ungratefulness get into you. Develop skills to be effective in a hostile environment without being hostile yourself. Every morning before going to work, remember those who sacrificed for you, so that when you walk in the door, you're filled with the right attitude.

We need to increase our capacity to work with different personalities. Be professional at all times. You're working with folks you don't normally associate with in your personal life. Increase your ability to work effectively with people you don't even like! Stop limiting your potential because of likes and dislikes. You may find a friend. Remember there is a purpose for everything and unlikable people will help to strengthen your leadership skills by increasing your coping skills and your ability to see things from different perspectives.

We need to understand that our work environment is not a place for emotional support. Your relationship with those in your personal life is different from your professional life. If you do decide to get close to someone on a personal level it should be in your private life. You need to stop telling folks on the job your business. You're at work to perform a task for which you are paid and to do that task professionally.

We don't need to find our security in pledging loyalty to cliques. Cliques are everywhere, on the job, in the church, even in families. Labels limit your usefulness. Learn to work with everybody but be labeled by nobody. Cliques categorize you into a particular group of people and limit your expressions. Don't go to public places trying to have personal friendships or emotional support. Get that from your personal life. Use all your gifts and talents. Dare to be unique.

Laughter and Humor as Therapy

Laughter in the workplace is not only therapeutic but has proven to boost morale, improve productivity, and increase job satisfaction. Humor helps to reduce the negative effects of stress. Humor allows you to be reflective, particularly when you find yourselves getting bogged down and burned out. Humor and laughter in the workplace incorporates a healthy balance between work and play, facilitate communication, enhance creativity and productivity at all levels and in your life.

Laughter may be the best medicine for both good health and optimal workplace performance and to improve your job performance if your work involves creativity and solving problems with more than one possible answer. Telling jokes can boost leaders' skills, too, if their managerial style is transformational meaning they urge workers to question norms or if it's laissez-faire, that is, they leave workers alone. Humor may have a different impact on "contingent reward" leaders, those who ask workers to obey explicit instructions since it distracts employees from following strict orders. Humor's effect depends on the task. If you're doing something creative, you might want to use it. Otherwise, you might not.

Many people do not realize that they should take their job seriously, but not themselves. Humor is an underutilized tool for inspiring leadership and loyalty, boosting morale and building team spirit. Humor is vital for peak performance and job satisfaction, as well as for thriving in today's complex, competitive world. In fact, a humorous outlook influences success. While it may sound strange, we do not laugh because we are happy, we are happy because we laugh. Laughter does not come from happiness; it comes from tension, stress and pain. Many of us laugh to keep from crying. Laughter and pain are a continuum. Laughing and crying are side-by-side, on the same level. Laughter is highly contagious. It affects us physically, our heart rate, hormones and our musculoskeletal system. Humor is intellectual, a way of viewing the world. You think certain things are funny and I think other things are funny because we have different senses of humor. Laughter, on the other hand, is universal. Laughter is not intellectual. We would have more opportunities to laugh if we did not think we have to agree on what is funny. Laughter does not need a reason to be. Laughter exists for its own sake. Laughter is unreasonable, illogical and irrational. Laughter helps ease the pressures of your work in a variety of settings and speeds up the "nine to five" clock. Laughter, balances fear and the internal chemistry of anger. Successful leaders develop that balance which enables them to overcome both fear and anger. For that matter, most of the time leaders should laugh at themselves rather and not at others.

Make them laugh is the new motto for a growing number of organizations trying to inject humor into the sometimes dull aspects of business. Stress, if not managed properly, reduces your life expectancy. I believe laughter provides the chemical rebalancing in our bodies which allows us to think more clearly and be all we can be. It helps people to rephrase the message, and we get more impact and reception. A good laugh helps restless employees endure a long presentation or get through a long day.

Laughter has always been a part of my life, even during the "poor old days". I am a student of humor, funny anecdotes, sayings and ideas. I support the notion that humor and laughter have not been used to their fullest potential as important tools for improving your people handling skills, including helping to resolve conflicts, open communications, relieve work tension and promote teamwork. Every successful leader utilizes humor in his or her leadership style. Laughter is a conscious process. Laughter helps us to enjoy life and feel better emotionally. I have learned one important thing about humor: we all may have a sense of humor, but our perspectives are quite different. While humor may diminish your authority, it is okay to laugh with co-workers. I cannot get along without humor. Never forget this message when working with people. If you want to defuse anger, lessen tension or simply be a "down-to-earth" regular person, then use humor whenever you can. Humor is innate, and it is a complement or companion to laughter. Humor is intellectual or a mental mind process, which allows each of us to determine what, is funny and what's not funny. Although something may be humorous, we do not have to laugh; some humor is sarcastic and not funny.

Fear creates feelings of isolation and separation, which will limit our ability to participate as team players. We become trapped in fear, afraid to laugh, without realizing that laughter is the one thing that will release us from fear. Look at it this way, if the work place was more fun, more people would come to work more often, and there would be less absenteeism and higher productivity. Laughter builds camaraderie and closeness, increases pleasure, productivity and loyalty, and is a great tension reducer for our bodies as well as our minds.

There is a saying that if fear is the lock, laughter is the key. Tension develops when we do not meet the group's expectations. Humor, based on embarrassment or light fear, is universal. Used appropriately, humor is a powerful leadership tool for improving the work environment. Humor helps relieve the tension that comes from living in this dog-eat-dog, the rich-get-richer and the poor-get-poorer society.

Humor helps your creativity. Laughter increases your ability to come up with innovative solutions to problems. A story joke like "There can't be life on Mars...Two tall people and a camel go into a bar..." is actually a problem solving word game. Humor may have the greatest value for people in lower positions in an organization. If you had to choose between two equally qualified jobs candidates, most would favor a person with a sense of humor. Humor is a valuable asset to an organization. People have different cultures, backgrounds and sensitivities, and humor delivered with an acid tongue and aimed at subordinates can be counterproductive. All of the isms (racism, sexism, classism, etc.) can be wrongly translated into hostile laughter.

Laughter is for everyone. Most leaders would agree that a good laugh feels good and humor has therapeutic qualities. Laughter is exercise; it increases the heart rate and stimulates circulation, works the diaphragm, abdominal wall and other muscle systems and increases production of the hormones that trigger the release of endorphins - the body's natural painkillers. Laughter provides a sense of balance and allows us to be intellectually free from our fears or threats. People rarely succeed at anything unless they have fun doing it. According to a number of researchers on stress reduction at work, the number-one stress buster was laughter.

We know that young people laugh more times a day than adults. If we could laugh more frequently, it is conceivable we could have the heart rate and blood pressure of a young person. Laughter alters blood chemistry to reduce pain, or simply dominates the nerve pathway, which normally would transmit the pain message to the brain. If you are a pain sufferer, try laughing, it is good medicine with no bad side effects. Laughter increases cerebrum activity, works through the mid-brain, and the hypothalamus is stimulated which plays a role in hormonal and epinephrine secretions and immune regulation. Lower epinephrine levels can reduce high blood pressure and help relieve other cardiovascular problems. When the diaphragm convulses during laughter, our internal organs get massaged which helps keep them functioning plump and juicy.

If we wait until we are happy to laugh, the world would be a quiet place. Without stress life would be dull and unexciting. Stress adds flavor, gusto, challenge and opportunity to life. Too much stress, however, can seriously affect your physical and mental well being. Stress is with us all the time. It comes from mental or emotional and physical activity. Too much emotional stress can cause physical illness such as high blood pressure, ulcers or even heart disease. Laughter is not likely to cause such ailments. The truth is that laughter can help you to relax and handle your mental or emotional stress more success fully.

For me, laughter and smiles works. Laughter is better than taking deep breaths or counting to ten. Laughter can provide psychological relief from tension, anxiety, anger, hostility, and emotional pain. Laughter can restore a sense of balance and eliminate the pressure of juggling. Laughter allows us to feel a degree of intellectual freedom from the people at work. If relief is what you are after, then laughter really is the best answer.

Laughter helps us to dispel anger, minimizing stressful events, and to cope with anxiety. Laughter can provide constructive information and techniques for dealing with stress. Laughter is a powerful healing tool. Laughter touches you from within, enhances your wisdom, invigorates and refreshes you. Laughter is a quality that we need to survive wherever we are with our careers and in life.

Laughter affects us emotionally. People often say they feel better after laughing. The beta-endorphin is a natural opiate in the brain that deadens pain. I believe laughter releases them. Laughter releases tension associated with what is happening to us. In other words, laughter reduces the severity of the problem and allows you to see solutions and help eliminate feelings of depression.

Laughter is a two step process, the joke is set up, and then the punch line is delivered. Physiologically, laughter (mirth) begins with brain arousal. During the process of a joke, brain activity heightens in anticipation or in recognition of the solution to the joke, in the same way it heightens in anticipation when confronted with a specific problem. Humor allows you to step back from a situation and to look at it as if you were a bystander, in this way a disastrous business trip seem funny after you get back to the office. For stress busting, the idea is to find ways to laugh at the situation while it is happening by playing up its absurdities. Use your imagination; consciously exaggerate the situation in your mind. If people stare at you because you seem to be laughing for no reason, then you should pretend to be reading a scandalous news report. It is much easier if you are naturally funny, but you do not have to be a master of one liners to be funny. Pick safe subjects. Your own embarrassing situation is safe. You will have people laughing with you, rather than at you. This kind of humor is a way of fighting stress by accepting our shortcomings.

Hurtful laughter should be avoided. Many people develop a shyness as a result of teasing in their past. Many people who were teased are afraid to laugh and have a dislike for other people's laughter. Nothing could be timelier than a good joke during stressful moments, especially if it is a true joke. Do not rush, especially to the punch line of the joke. Try not to tell long jokes with weak puns, or word plays. Find a joke that is funny, learn it and go out and tell it. Give the gift of humor, if you have it, share it. Laughter is a bonding device.

We should make humor a part of our leadership style, be lighthearted at work, enjoy our work more, get along better with people in our work place and improve the delivery of customer services. We should seek out people we can laugh with and use them as a valuable resource. We should use humor in negotiations as a good business strategy. If you do, you will succeed every time.

Networking 101 Win Relationships

Even if we provide one of the most valuable services imaginable, without an ongoing and ever-increasing number of new, quality prospects, we'll eventually run out of people with whom to share the benefits. As a result, networking and developing profitable win/win relationships with people we meet is critical.

Successful networking requires that you know how to ask questions, not just any questions, but specifically, "feel-good" questions. These are questions designed to put your conversation partner at ease, and begin the rapport-building process. Feel-good questions are simply questions that make your new prospect/potential referral-source feel good about themselves, about the conversation, and about you. This is important because if "all things being equal, people will do business with, and refer business to, those people they know, like and trust." There are a number of "Feel-good" type questions. For example, how did you get started in the 'widget' business?" This is called the "Movie-of-the-Week" question because most people love the opportunity to "tell their story" to someone.

Networking marketing starts when you begin to establish a nice rapport with your new prospect. Now it's time for the "One key question." Also, since you are asking for help in identifying their prospects, they will gladly supply you with an answer. Nothing builds trust and credibility with a prospect more than actually referring business to people who make them feel special and important whenever possible.

Hopefully, you have gotten your prospect's business card. Whenever meeting new people, the above questions will help you to very quickly build your prospect list with high-quality people. The typical person knows about two hundred and fifty people. Sales are frequently developed through the relationships we have created with other people. Networking functions provide the opportunity to expand our contact list, particularly when we create and nurture quality relationships. It is not enough to visit a networking group, talk to dozens of people and gather as many business cards possible. However, every networking function has tremendous potential for new business leads. There are strategies to make networking profitable.

First, choose the right networking group or event. The best results come from attending the appropriate networking events for your particular industry. This should include trade shows, conferences, and associations dedicated to your type of business. For example, if your target market is a Fortune 500 company, it does not make sense to join a group whose primary membership consists of individual business owners. Focus on quality contacts versus quantity. Most people have experienced the person who, while talking to you, keeps his eyes roving around the room, seeking his or her next victim. This individual is more interested in passing out and collecting business cards than establishing a relationship. A good approach is to make between two and five new contacts at each networking meeting you attend. Focus on the quality of the connection and people will become much more trusting of you.

Make sure you make a positive first impression. Factors that influence this initial impact are your handshake, facial expressions, eye contact, interest in the other person and your overall attentiveness. Develop a great handshake, approach people with a natural, genuine smile and make good eye contact. Listen carefully to their name. Many people do not speak clearly or loudly enough and others are very nervous at networking events. Develop a ten second introduction as well as a thirty second presentation. For example; "I work with boutique retailers to help them increase their sales and profits." Most people drop the ball here. Mention something from your conversation and express your interest to keep in contact. Always include a business card in your correspondence. Networking does produce results.

Principles

- Your long-term happiness is a road map pursuing that next goal, going after the things you value and enjoying journey to your dreams, rather than having the goal itself.

- Never quit, there are going to be ups and downs and failures in life, plan to succeed.

9
HEALTH, WELLNESS AND SUCCESS

"Success is to be measured not so much by the position that one has reached in life as by the obstacles which he has overcome while trying to succeed."

— Booker T. Washington,
Then Darkness Fled: The Liberating Wisdom of Booker T. Washington

Interactions Between Your Mind and Body

In earlier systems of medicine in Africa treatment has been made with the view that mind, body and soul are linked together as a whole and should not be seen as isolated from each other. With that in mind, your overall health and fitness combines physical, emotional, mental and spiritual aspects of your being. Mind-body healing approach that enhances each person's self-knowledge focusing on the interactions between the brain, mind, body and the ways in which emotional, mental, social, spiritual and behavioral factors affect us as a whole. Mind-body medicine is a term that demonstrates physical, chemical, mental and spiritual interconnectedness, and currently encompasses a wide variety of techniques such as biofeedback, relaxation training, meditation, guided imagery, spiritual healing, and many other interventions.

There is a connection between your own values and interactions with others, and feeling good about yourself. For mind wellness, you need mental stimulation and challenges, such as reading, problem solving or being creative. For emotional wellness, you need to take care of yourself and nurture yourself by setting aside time for yourself to express, deal with and release your emotions. For spiritual wellness, you need to be grounded, spend time alone in quiet reflection, enjoy nature, pray or engage in some type of religious ritual, believe a higher power or life wonders to nurture your spirit. For you physical wellness, you need to listen to your body, be healthy with good nutrition , warmth, comfort, exercise, physical activity, sleep, self-care and body treatments, hygiene, rest and relaxation.

Exercise is an underutilized means for achieving overall wellness. As a former athlete, I have been accustomed to being fit. Exercise is a factor of good health and will help you to actually sleep when you go to bed, maintain optimal weight, improve your immune system for disease prevention, and improve your ability to think. I attribute much of my success to being in excellent physical shape. Action is essential to your well-being. Most people know about the feel-good endorphins released by the brain during physical exercise. Balance in your work and personal life as well as nutrition is the key.

Forgive yourself when you don't measure up and forgive others when they need it. The ability to find the humor in the human situation is a definite plus. Hearty laughter gives a sense of deep relaxation, and tends to soften your perspective on problems. It also eases pain.

People who exercise regularly have better health, but only a small percentage of U.S. adults engage in regular exercise, with some social groups, such as people with lower incomes and women, having even lower rates. People eat for many different reasons but hunger isn't at the top of the list. Although we all have times when we soothe our egos or marital, romantic, or family problems hurt emotions with a tub of ice cream or a bag of chips, emotional eating involves deeper connections with food. Similar to the way others use alcohol or cigarettes, emotional eaters use food as a way of dealing with various feelings, including anger, sadness, and loneliness. Due to social stigma, we do not like to talk about emotional eating which is increasing among people in all walks of life. There are many reasons why people resort to food as a comforter, but, old habits die hard. Weight is a major problem in maintaining good overall health. Many people battle the bulge every day and hope that they will find a diet that works for them. You don't need expensive gym memberships to exercise. You can use your emotional intelligence by tricking your brain into thinking that you are full, change your life style and exercise. You can create the body you want based on your positive exercise goals and giving yourself what you want, not only in the area of food or eating, but in the larger arena of your life. It is rare to achieve a positive outcome from a negative motivation; if that were possible, the most negative people would be the happiest, but, it just doesn't work that way. People develop a shopping habit or some other addiction to try to fill a need within themselves. Most people call these feelings "urges," and go through life trying to satisfy their urges, believing that their satisfaction is what will bring them happiness. But the satisfaction of our desires is not the way to bring about lasting happiness. Rather than try to avoid the feelings, we need to change the way we relate to them so that they are not causing us discomfort. By learning how to feed yourself with things that are self-loving and nurturing, you will stop eating more food than you need, lose weight, reach and maintain your ideal weight without dieting or deprivation. Just eating less will help you loose more weight and keep money in your pocket. You want to do this so that we too can live healthy lives with self-esteem, self-confidence and self-worth. You need to identify what beliefs, behavioral scripts and old tapes you need to change so that you can improve your relationship with food. With food you have three choices: to eat it, to eat less of it or not to eat it at all. The choice is yours. As fitness and weight loss expert Bob Greene says, "The root of most people's weight problems, or any problems that relate to lack of motivation, is buried deep within. For long-term success, spend the time to make yourself emotionally healthy before you even think about adjusting your diet or joining a gym."

Every time I wanted to stop exercising, I started to think about my friends and supporter who are rooting for me at the end of the finishing line. That helps to keep me focused on exercising for at least another 30 minutes. In writing this book I remember saying, "just two more chapters and I can take a break." "Once I have completed these projects, I can get away for relaxation without any worries." Do the above statements sound familiar to you? If the answer is yes, you are probably one of the many people practicing the art of daily motivation in your lives.

Sticking with your exercise program regularly and consistently is your best bet for overall health. While there's no specific danger in starting and stopping, over and over again, it's important to set personal goals and identify what motivates you to exercise. For some, it's disease prevention. If a close family member has been affected by heart disease, diabetes, arthritis, osteoporosis, or cancer, we avoid the same path. Regular exercise reduces your risk of developing these and other diseases and will help you maintain a healthy body weight. For others, living longer is a motivator. Research has shown that exercise may extend the years of your life. It can greatly enhance your quality of living, too, by making regular day-to-day physical activities such as climbing stairs, carrying groceries, and vacuuming easier.

Regardless of where we are, we need to get started. How you start an exercise program may greatly determine whether you stick with it. We can begin by setting realistic goals. We shouldn't try to run a marathon or lose ten pounds in a month. We can take little steps, begin slowly and try a number of different exercises. We can limit the length of each session. We can use visualization daily and picture ourselves enjoying our workout and then feeling great when we've finished. We can schedule exercise just like we do other social activities and make it a top priority in our life. We can write it down on our calendar and keep a daily exercise log. We can identify one exercise that we enjoy doing on most days. If you're traveling, maintain some kind of routine. Find a fitness center at the hotel, go for a swim, or take a long walk. You can also try strengthening exercises such as push-ups, sit-ups, calf raises, and lunges.

Don't feel guilty when you miss a session or two. Negative feelings will only hinder your motivation. Getting back on track will make you feel better. If boredom is hindering your routine, try doing new exercises, pick a new sport, or recruit an exercise partner. The key is finding something you like and sticking with it. Distractions can be a resource not a problem. This includes reading, listening to music, or watching television while you work out can help keep you motivated. Try exercising at a different time of day, or break up a workout schedule to include aerobic exercise in the morning and strength training at night. For some, buying an exercise tape that you find entertaining is a good idea, scheduling several sessions with a personal trainer or joining an exercise class that has a lively instructor is a winner. Whatever you decide to do, it's important to not get discouraged if you miss a week or two of exercise. It's never too late to start again. When your program gets derailed, try to figure out what went wrong and learn from your mistakes. Even if there's been a long lapse in your sessions, you should do your best to get back to regular exercise as soon as you can. Your doctor should play a primary role in guiding your physical well-being.

In order to help avoid serious illness or injury if you have certain medical conditions, it is recommended that you consult a physician before beginning an exercise program.

For Mind Sake, Listen to Your Body

Everyone has emotional stress, short or long-term, discrimination, a life-threatening illness, or divorce. Stressful events affect your health on many levels. Long-term stress is real and can increase your risk for some health problems, like depression. Both short and long-term stress can have effects on your body. Emotions provide clues to your overall health. For example, stress can take on many different forms, and can contribute to symptoms of illness. Common symptoms include headache, sleep disorders, difficulty concentrating, short-temper, upset stomach, job dissatisfaction, low morale, depression, and anxiety.

As we explore the extraordinary interplay of energies between the many aspects of our personality, our needs, unconscious reactions, repressed emotions, aspirations and fears with the functioning of our body, our physical system and its capacity to maintain itself, we realize how very wise our body is. Our body is always silently speaking. We need to check and examine our body with our awareness. Our body is the ground, symbol and image of our life, the appearance or expression of our existence or reality. If your body is both physical and spiritual, and there is a blending of physical with spiritual, disassociation or divorce is impossible. With your body and mind being in balance, you will be in harmony.

Our health is a state of complete physical, mental and social well-being, and not merely the absence of disease or infirmity. Our greatest wealth is not material things or status, it is our health. For many of us, life expectancy would grow by leaps and bounds if green vegetables smelled as good as bacon.

Our body image involves our perception of who we are our imagination, emotions, and physical sensations. Body image is not static but ever-changing not inborn, but learned. Our body image is sensitive to changes in our mood, environment, and physical experience. Our psychological boundaries develop early in life, based on how we are held and touched or not held and touched. People who have been abused may feel terrible pain and shame or loathing associated to their body and resist close content.

Most people want a positive reception, to be thought of favorably, or to be noticed. We all seek attention and appreciation in one way or another. Attention or self-awareness includes listening for and responding to internal cues such as hunger, satiety, and fatigue. Appreciation refers to enjoying the pleasures your body can provide. The power of love to change our bodies is well-known and celebrated, built into folklore, common sense, and everyday experience. Throughout history, "tender loving care" has uniformly been recognized as a valuable element in our overall health and healing.

Too many of us have become obsessed with our outward appearance. I am careful about reading health books; I could die of a misprint. Physical ills are the taxes laid upon our life; some are taxed higher, and some lower, but all pay something. My physician reminds me, "You should be made to understand that you must take charge of your own life. Don't take your body to the doctor as if he (the doctor's office) were a repair shop." If you have health, you probably will be happy, and if you have health and happiness, you have all the wealth you need, even if it is not all you want.

Most of our ills are food and stress related. Stress experts believe that eating a healthy diet helps combat stress. A well balanced diet is crucial in preserving your health and helps to reduce stress. When you are stressed your bodies produce stress hormones, which release fatty acids and sugars to help you cope. When this happens, your blood sugar levels can become disrupted. Blood sugars help us regulate our body's fuel requirements, what we eat and drink. Some people eat more when they feel stressed while others feel they cannot face food. If you do not eat, your blood sugar level drops, causing reactions in the nervous system, which can create feelings of anxiety.

Some experts in the stress management field believe that if your regular diet contains large amounts of refined sugars such as chocolate, cake, biscuits and sugar-based foods or is low in protein or fat, or you are using too many stimulants, such as coffee or cola-based drinks, this may aggravate stress reactions in certain people.

Many medical doctors and government agencies recommend that people reduce the amount of red meat and overall percentage of fats in their diet. As a result, people have cut down or eliminated red meat from their diet. While poultry and fish do have less saturated fat than beef and pork, they're still high in fat and have cholesterol. For your body's sake, listen to it, eat well, deal with life stress and let's live.

Nutritional Knowledge, Health and Wellness

We all eat based on our personal food choices. Our food choices are controlled or influenced by both our individual and collective behavior. This includes our physiological state, food preferences, nutritional knowledge, perceptions of healthy eating and psychological factors. At the beginning and later in life, we are influenced by our eating behavior. Dietary quality in nutrition appears to decrease with age. This is perhaps a function of our emotional and social development that provides us with more control over our food choices and is influenced by our food preferences and nutritional knowledge. Food preferences are individual and may be physiological such as our preferences for sweets and aversions for bitter tastes. Our culture plays a role and may determine our food preferences.

Many people have a general understanding of the connections between food choice and health. High awareness of nutrition and health is associated with better food and nutrient intakes. Nutritional knowledge relates to our perceptions of what we eat, healthy eating. Perceptions of healthy eating are defined by our culture in terms of meanings of food and health. Individual psychological factors that affect our eating include personality traits such as self-esteem, body image and restrained eating (chronic dieting), as well as mood and focus of attention. Our food choices affect our psychological well-being. Our physical and social environment including our family and peers affects our eating. Exposure to numerous advertisements and promotions influences healthy eating such as our food preferences and perceptions of healthy eating. Slick advertisements give priority to distorted nutritional messages designed to sell individual products, not to promote a total diet. Studies have consistently shown that people within higher social class, generally defined using education as an indicator, rather than income or occupation have healthier diets. This means eating more fruit, vegetables and low-fat, as well as fewer fats and oils, and less meat. An income threshold refers to the likelihood that, beneath the threshold, income is the most important determinant of consumption; a socio-economic gradient suggests that other determinants, especially education, are also likely to be important. It seems very likely that socioeconomic is a contributor to your diet, as well as income for some food groups. Nutritional inequalities exist.

We have heard it before, "you are what you eat" and a healthy diet is only as healthy as the food that is eaten. It is therefore important to take into account your likes and dislikes and your ability to manage certain foods. Consider ways of preparing food to stimulate your interest, particularly if your appetite is poor. Remember, eating healthily does not mean that certain foods have to be avoided. My approach is...everything in moderation including what you like is the key to enjoying food and staying fit and well.

Foods contain combinations of nutrients and other healthful substances. For example, oranges provide vitamin C. Some people eat vegetarian diets for reasons of culture, belief, or health. Most vegetarians eat milk products and eggs, and as a group, these are called lacto-ovo-vegetarians. Vegans eat only food of plant origin and maintain a healthy weight. To maintain a healthy body weight, people must balance the amount of calories in the foods and drinks they consume with the amount of calories the body uses.

To decrease calorie intake, eat a variety of foods that are low in calories but high in nutrients. It is important to check the Nutrition Facts Label on the foods you eat. The following has proven to be helpful to me:

- Eat less fat and fewer high-fat foods.

- Eat smaller portions and limit second helpings of foods high in fat and calories.

- Eat more vegetables and fruits without fats and sugars added in preparation or at the table.

- Eat plenty of grains, vegetables, and fruits.

I have found that grain products, vegetables, and fruits are key parts of my varied diet. In terms of fiber, there are different types of fiber in foods, choose a variety of foods daily. Choose a diet low in fat, saturated fat, and cholesterol. Some dietary fat is needed for good health. Fats supply energy and essential fatty acids and promote absorption of the fat-soluble vitamins A, D, E, and K. More Americans are now eating less fat, saturated fat, and cholesterol containing goods than in the recent past. Still, many people continue to eat high-fat diets. This guideline emphasizes the continued importance of choosing a diet with less total fat, saturated fat, and cholesterol.

I try to avoid high-fat foods. Some foods and food groups are higher in fat than others. Fats and oils, and some types of desserts and snack foods that contain fat provide calories but few other nutrients. Choose a diet that provides no more than 30 percent of total calories from fat. The upper limit on the grams of fat in your diet will depend on the calories you need. Cutting back on fat can help you consume fewer calories. For example, at 2,000 calories per day, the suggested upper limit of calories from fat is about 600 calories (65 grams of fat x 9 calories per gram = about 600 calories).

Saturated fat-Fats contain both saturated and unsaturated (monounsaturated and polyunsaturated) fatty acids. Saturated fat raises blood cholesterol more than other forms of fat. Reducing saturated fat to less than 10 percent of calories will help you lower your blood cholesterol level. The fats from meat, milk, and milk products are the main sources of saturated fats in most diets. Many bakery products are also sources of saturated fats. Vegetable oils supply smaller amounts of saturated fat.

Monounsaturated and polyunsaturated fat include olive and canola oils are particularly high in monounsaturated fats; most other vegetable oils, nuts, and high-fat fish are good sources of polyunsaturated fats. Both kinds of unsaturated fats reduce blood cholesterol when they replace saturated fats in the diet. Monounsaturated and polyunsaturated fat sources should replace saturated fats within this limit. I believe that we should choose a low cholesterol diet. Dietary cholesterol comes from animal sources such as egg yolks, meat (especially organ meats such as liver), poultry, fish, and higher-fat milk products. Many of these foods are also high in saturated fats. Choosing foods with less cholesterol and saturated fat will help lower your blood-pressure and blood-cholesterol levels.

It make seen to avoid too much sugar. Sugars are simple carbohydrates. Dietary carbohydrates also include starch and fiber, which are complex carbohydrates. Sugars and starches occur naturally in many foods that supply other nutrients. Examples of these foods include milk, fruits, some vegetables, breads, cereals, beans, and grains. Avoid too much sodium. Sodium occurs naturally in foods, usually in small amounts.

It is very important to use natural, unrefined, often brown sugars instead of white sugars or sweetners. To digest refined white sugar, your body has to use a lot of energy and it works as a stimulant. A stimulant is a substance that quickly changes a symptom in an unnatural way. Many people in Western society live on stimulation. We use stimulation to make us feel good. If you try to control a symptom with stimulants, the cause of that symptom will remain. The core of a problem will never be solved by using stimulants. The number of stimulants we use is endless. Sweetners make you crave for sugar about 30 minutes after consumption so you end up robbing the cookie jar. Unrefined brown sugars are natural and provide you with energy. They include brown sugar - cane sugar.

If you keep your food in balance, your body will detoxify itself. Stimulants cannot give the body what it needs. Only natural food can promote a healthy and thus happy physiological function. You could look at it this way: the only natural way to feel good is the one that is a by-product of a normally functioning body that is producing sufficient energy at the cellular level. Any other way to feel good is phony and a result of stimulants, regardless of how innocent these stimulants may look. Your body detoxifies itself all day and for the biggest part during your sleep. It makes sense to eat fruits and vegetables only during the day when your body is detoxifying. Your body has to dispose of the toxic elements it receives from stimulants, nutrition and pollution. This information is not intended to be a substitute for professional medical advice or treatment. It s recommended that you get a full physical and consult your medical professional.

Everyday Behavior and Lifestyle Practice

We need a certain amount of daily inspiration to energize us. If stress or tension accumulates and is not relieved it can stress our body's immune system and trigger health problems. There are many ways to relieving stress by improving our diet, increasing exercise, or just making time for ourselves. If you were told you only had one day to live, what would be your priority in terms of what you should be giving time to and help you feel less stressed. With lifestyle changes you can make a world of difference to your stress levels. Smiling is easy and can help improve your mood and the people around you. Since being happy and smiling is a de-stressor, you should plan time for personal pleasure and enjoying. Laughter's contagious and can help reduce blood pressure, relax muscle tension and release an enzyme that protects your stomach from forming ulcers. So take time to go out and have fun with friends. Practice breathing exercises by taking deep breaths regularly throughout the day. Deep breathing helps prevent the body turning on the stress response mechanism. Try and build deep breaths into your routine. Eat well. Foods high in fat or sugar and alcohol over stimulate the body and trigger the body's stress mechanism. Nutrients are also used more quickly when you're stressed. Eat plenty of vitamin B (green vegetable, fruit, and nuts) vitamin C in fruit juices, and complex carbohydrates oats, pasta and rice. Healthy fruits such as blackberries, strawberries and oranges are rich in vitamin C and can help boost the Adrenaline stores in your body, which are lost when stress kicks in. Even five minutes exercise a day can be beneficial. Exercise is a great stress buster, as feel-good chemicals released in the brain help to keep energy levels going and help defend the body against stress-inducing toxin and free radical damage. Many of us feel overloaded by everyday tasks and we need to organize ourselves better so that we manage more effectively and reduce our stress levels.

Make a plan of action and prioritize it into what's urgent and vital, then important and finally things that can be done at your leisure. Regular physical activity is essential for overall wellness and success in life. Incorporating fruits, vegetables, protein and whole grains in your diet every day can help you stay on track to a healthier lifestyle necessary to achieving your dreams. Studies show that relaxing can help reduce the effects of stress, assist in immune function and lower blood pressure. A few largely preventable risk factors including how we eat, drink and move account for most of the disease burden and chronic diseases such as cardiovascular conditions, diabetes, stroke, cancers and respiratory diseases. It takes only a few minutes a day to become more physically active. If you do no t have 30 minutes in your schedule for an exercise break, try to find two 15-minute periods or even three 10-minute periods. These exercise breaks will soon become a habit you can't live without. You can improve your health and quality of life by including moderate amounts of physical activity and proper nutrition in your daily lives. Physical activity and nutrition are two of many everyday behaviors that affect health. Emotional Intelligence also plays a central role for our emotions in medical health. Research has identified the links between the immune system and the central nervous system and connects emotional states to illness. People who experienced chronic anxiety, long periods of sadness and pessimism, unremitting tension or incessant hostility, relentless cynicism or suspiciousness, have been found to have double the risk of disease-including asthma, arthritis, headaches, peptic ulcers, and heart disease.

Everyday, newspapers report the concerns about youth fitness, childhood obesity and the low levels of physical activity and exercise engaged in by many adults. Sadly, only about one-half of U.S. young people (ages 12-21 years) regularly participate in vigorous physical activity and about one-fourth participate in no vigorous physical activity. As we get older, we participate in physical activity less and less. Time changes all of us and it is difficult to overestimate just how important physical activity is to our health.

We know that higher levels of regular physical activity play a vital role in your overall well-being and are associated with lower death or mortality rates for both older and younger adults. Regular physical activity or cardio respiratory fitness decreases the risk of cardiovascular disease mortality in general and of coronary heart disease mortality in particular. Regular physical activity is associated with a decreased risk of colon cancer. Regular physical activity lowers the risk of developing non-insulin-dependent diabetes mellitus. Regular physical activity is necessary for maintaining normal muscle strength, joint structure, and joint function. Physical activity may favorably affect body fat distribution. Physical activity appears to relieve symptoms of depression and anxiety and helps to improve our mood.

Your physical health depends on educating yourself about what your body needs. What nutrients does your body need and in what amounts? What exercises can you perform for best results and without damaging your body? It's important to know and understand what your body needs, and a visit your doctor or health care provider can provide that information. We need aerobic and anaerobic activity to achieve and maintain physical fitness. Aerobic activity includes exercises that stimulate your cardio respiratory system (mainly your heart and lungs, but other organs as well). These activities include walking, jogging, swimming, and of course, aerobics. Anaerobic activity includes exercises that stimulate your skeleto-muscular system (mainly your bones, cartilage, and muscles, which support your organs). These activities include weight-lifting and calisthenics, such as sit-ups or crunches. Sports, games, and gyms offer the opportunity to get this type of activity. Simply walking around the block, running around the yard, or climbing steps will help. Just remember, before you start a formal exercise program, talk to your doctor to find out what types of activities are best for your body.

Too many of us forget that we need to eat and drink well. Eating well can mean different things to different people. Some people require special diets due to food allergies or illnesses. Your age, gender, size, activity level, medical history, and medication usage, in addition to other such factors, all influence what type of diet is right for you. Again, it's important to talk to your health care provider about what your body needs. In general, your body requires six essential nutrients. These are vitamins, minerals, proteins, fats, carbohydrates, and water. Your body gets or manufactures these nutrients through what you consume. Since no two bodies have the exact same nutritional needs, you should consult your physician or nutritionist to determine the diet that's right for you. If you want to eat well, maximize your intake of whole foods, such as fresh or frozen vegetables and fruit, and grains, such as oats, minimize your intake of processed foods, such as items made with white flour, hydrogenated oil, or white table sugar. Keep fat intake to less than 30% of your total daily calories, minimize your intake of saturated fat, and consume salt, alcohol, and sugars (such as white table sugar, brown sugar, corn syrup, maltose, and molasses) in moderation.

We all need to sleep well. Just as we need aerobic and anaerobic activity, our body also need to rest. During sleep, your body regenerates cells, circulates nutrients, and gives your muscles and organs rest. Different people require different amounts of sleep. Get to know what your body requires, and manage your time so that your body gets the rest it needs to help you be your best when you awaken. Many studies indicate that we are more attentive and productive after getting an adequate amount of sleep. If you want to sleep well, avoid caffeine five hours before you go to sleep, keep the room in which you sleep dark, avoid alcohol before going to bed and avoid exercising three hours before going to sleep.

We know that mental therapy helps us to release anger, but it can only take you so far. Physical exercise can help many people let off steam, but it may not remove deep-seated anger. The most effective process is when you can combine both the mental and physical effort. This is when you do a particular physical activity along with the mental intention of releasing the anger.

Stop and take a breath. Now take a slow, strong, long breath. Feel your heart slow down its hectic rhythm. Feel your head clear, keep breathing. Inhaling allows oxygen to enter your body, feed your cells, and purify your blood and organs from toxins. Exhaling allows your body to eliminate those toxins. Breathe deeply from your abdomen and get the most out of the air around you. When you are tense, nervous, anxious, angry, confused, frustrated, sad, scared, breathe and regain your sense of self, balance and being. I know you will say, it's hard to do. That why, we need to practice. We need to make breathing and physical activity a part of our everyday life. Just by doing this, we can change ourselves, our lives and our communities.

Principles

- Your positive thoughts create a domino effect working consistently with your purpose to be supportive of your overall health and happiness.

- Your optimistic purpose driven thinking provides significant health benefits.

10
CULTIVATING GRATITUDE

"Success doesn't come to you...you go to it."

— Marva Collins, *Marva Collins' Way*

Gratitude and Self-Reflection

They say, "You don't know a good thing until it's gone." Gratitude arises from how we look at things. It is the natural feeling that comes from truly appreciating the people and things in your life. It is also something you can learn. Gratitude is a choice. It doesn't depend upon circumstances or something that you don't have control over. It really becomes an attitude that you can choose that makes your life better and for other people. When things are going fine, gratitude enables you to appreciate those things. When things are going not so well, gratitude enables you to get over them and see it as a temporary set-back.

For many people, it takes failure or tragedy to bring about a sense of humbleness. For some, humility isn't cultivated because it may be viewed as a sign of weakness. But humility is power; it's having the ability to recognize life's blessings and accept them with gratitude. Purpose comes from doing what we were born to do, from following our heart and trusting your joy as a guide. Your enthusiasm and passion come as a result of caring about what you do. Imagine getting up each day knowing you are doing exactly what you love to do, are passionate about, and can't wait to start doing. The most joyful people are often those who have a purpose or a mission that motivates, inspires and drives them forward. Whatever you focus on you'll get more of. If you're focusing on lack, you're going to get more lack. If you focus on abundance, you're going to get more abundance. We need to find something in our life right now to be grateful for because at that point we will start to attract more things to be grateful for.

It's a fact. We know that we can't control external circumstances. All we can do is balance ourselves so that if something traumatic happens, you need to know how to balance yourselves very quickly. So, shifting your situation to the positive allows you to actually change your life.

Gratitude is not an imaginary idea. It is a sense of appreciating what you feel in response to a gift. Gratitude may be viewed as an emotion, a quality of character that gives you a positive perspective on life, a coping response or even a skill. Fostering the quality of forgiveness can also help you experience a good life. Forgiveness requires giving up long held resentment, constant negative judgment of oneself and others and sometimes even the ability to get along with those you dislike. Forgive and appreciate, be grateful for what you have.

Be Focused, Joyful and Grateful

We were born to be joyful. The choice is ours, we can choose to be more joyful and let our joy incredibly impact our life and those around us. As we work at being joyful, it becomes a habit. Happiness depends on what is happening in your environment but joy comes from within. Joy is an attitude of thankfulness and is a constant regardless of your circumstances. We need to be thankful for the little things and sooner or later you will foster a mental attitude of gratitude and thankfulness. Happy people are grateful people. Being Joyful doesn't mean that your life is easier. Joyful people recognize goodness in the midst of their own suffering and in the midst of human suffering.

Joyful people feel the joy from inside and share it with others with their kind words, their smile and their presence. You must find joy and learn to be joyful every day. Joy is the word for the feeling when you are in control of your life. Joy is the inner feeling that tells you everything will be all right, so be happy and enjoy yourself. Your ability to laugh at your mistakes and shortcomings is guaranteed to bring joy into your day. Your life may appear ridiculous, don't take life too seriously, laugh at it and find laughter and humor in each day. Laughter and tears come from the same place, within us. You must become a giver not a taker and find joy in serving as you move towards your dreams.

Too many people are waiting for that perfect moment to act on their dreams. The only perfect people are in the cemetery. You need to stop comparing your life with the lives of other people. Be grateful and thankful for what you have and express your gratitude every day. In your life, there is always something to be thankful for. And when you are thankful, joy will naturally follow. Don't wait, find joy and live in the moment. You can be joyful right now. Take each moment of your life for what it is, find joy in your life and celebrate in the moment. Life is like s superhighway with joy in one lane and sorrow in the other. On your highway, you will find things that can make you both happy and sad. The trick is in knowing that both come at the same time. Joy is rooted in gratitude and the only person limiting your capacity for joy is you.

We all need joy in our lives. Joy starts from the inside and is reflected on the outside. Although the intent of our inner voice is to help us to succeed, often, our inner voice can be unforgiving and our own worst critic. We really don't have to spend time identifying our faults; our friends will take care of that. But we can ignore them. To defuse your inner self-critic, you need to recognize when your inner critic is speaking. You must realize that your abilities wither under your own constant faultfinding and flourish when your inner voice and self-talk provide you with words of encouragement. You should never react emotionally to criticism. Each time you spread joy to another, the positive power of that joy begins to multiply. Your joy is infectious. Joy can light the darkest days. Give your heart the experience of joy...and let your joy expand.

If we define a dream as something that you want, that has passion and meaning for us and that we believe in, then we all have dreams. Even if we tend to be unrealistic, we still have dreams. Whether we have a dream or are in need of a new one, whether our dream is for ourselves, our community or the world, having a dream is our chance to act. On those days when there is no evidence that your dream is possible, much less a good idea, we need to be resolved and focus on our strengths and not our weaknesses. We need to be committed to our dreams to help us change old habits and boost our confidence so that difficult changes ahead will seem easy.

We need to make a decision that will help us to imagine the dream we have will actually come true. We need to imagine transforming our attitude and maintain optimism daily. We need to imagine escaping our present life and living the life of our dreams. We need to imagine having the respect and admiration that we desire from others. We need to imagine accomplishing the things we desire, making the kind of money we want, and developing successful relationships. We need imagine ourselves at the top of our profession or field with no goal going unfulfilled. We need to imagine what it would be like to know how to stay motivated all the time, making a difference in the world around us and leaving a lasting legacy.

To achieve all that we imagine, we need to focus on our strengths and not our weaknesses. We need to focus on our life, present not our past life. We need to build a personal action plan for happiness as unique as we are. We need goals. Most people have a love-hate relationship with goals. They love them because they are such a great idea and a wonderful way to motivate us to achieve, as well as evaluate our progress, but hate them because more often than not they go unattained and simply frustrate us. This isn't what our goals should do.

To achieve all that we imagine, we need to narrow our focus. Start small, pick two or three areas that we want to work on. Too many of us say to ourselves, "I want to do this, and this, and this, and this..." and we end up doing nothing! Most of what we do throughout our day can be done without a lot of mental or emotional exertion, but change isn't one of them. So we need to focus on a few things and get some success. Pick an area: physical, intellectual, emotional, spiritual, financial, or relational.

To achieve all that we imagine, we need to keep the long-term in mind, but set our sights on achieving our goals in the short-term. In the physical, for example, we imagine we want to lose twenty five pounds, we will in the long-term. The key is not to think about losing twenty five pounds within a year but to think about losing five pounds by a certain period. You can sabotage yourself by saying, "Oh well, I still have twelve months to lose the twenty five pounds" because eventually that twelve becomes two months to lose twenty five pounds and stress sets you up to fail. Secondly, shorter goals give us regular victories instead of regular progress. Progress feels good, but achieving a goal is inspiring. We need to reward ourselves when we achieve the goal. When we lose the 5 pounds by a certain date, we need treat ourselves to a mini-vacation. This puts a little fun back into the process of self-control and self-discipline. Instead of saying "I am going to lose twenty five pounds," say "I am going to lose ten pounds." But don't just say, "I am going to lose ten pounds." Say, "I am going to lose ten pounds by April 1st." Make your goal specific and measurable.

Post your resolutions where you will see them every day. This will keep the resolution in the front of your mind at all times. Instead of forgetting that you are trying to lose weight and ordering a big, thick porterhouse, you will have been reminded earlier that day that you need to eat something on the lighter side. It will help your will beat your desire.

Find an encouraging person as an insurance policy, someone you respect, to keep you accountable to your resolution. This person should ask you, at an interval established by the both of you, how it is going. They must be the encouraging type, though. If you are struggling, they may say, "Well, that's okay, try again tomorrow." If you are doing well, they can say, "That's fantastic. Let's talk in a couple of days." You will look forward to theses types of inspirations. Find a partner, someone who is trying to accomplish the same or similar thing. Just make sure that they really want to change, or they will end up complaining about how hard it is and you will both fail.

If you are trying to lose weight, you might list the benefits such as feeling better, better self-esteem, longer life, being able to comfortably fit in all your clothes and looking younger again. If you want to stop smoking, the benefits may be better breath, no more brown fingers, less wrinkles on your face, no more red eyes, no more smelly clothes, and longer life.

Identifying benefits will help you see what you will get from accomplishing your goals or resolution. Don't get caught in the trap of all or nothing. Reward yourself on your journey.

We often attempt to live our lives backwards. Too many of us live in the past, thinking of the "good old days," happiness or pleasures that we enjoyed a long time ago, becoming nostalgic and wishing for those "good old days." As for the future, others dwell on future plans from "sun up to sun down" until it affects their eating and sleeping patterns, not able eat well or get enough sleep. Focusing too much on the future can cause us to worry needlessly, thinking about an impending problem, so much that we cannot concentrate on what we are presently doing. Too much past or future recalling, observing, or perceiving is not healthy. Living in the present moment means living with passion, skillfully in the present. When we live in the present, there will be no regrets when we think back about the past. We need to keep our mind engaged and focused on the present. For example, when we get angry, your mind can tell us: "Hey, check yourself. You are getting angry. You better get a hold of yourself and relax." There is no need to say or do anything which you will regret later. When you are mindful of your thoughts, you can see and identify your anger. With that insight and understanding, you can be aware of the dangers of venting to anger. The same is true for worry and anxiety. We can notice how worrisome we are becoming, how poorly we are applying what we know about ourselves and have learned in life. You can check your negative thinking patterns. You can adjust and correct your attitudes. If you try to stay more in the present by being aware of your true self, pay more attention to whatever you do, you can check your worrying mind. We are here now, in the present, we must learn to live from moment to moment, day to day, do the best we can to address problems as they comes along, and not give in to nerve-racking worry. By doing this, we will be living well.

The main point is to not to get trapped by self-indulgence, anger and delusion. Your self development mission is to cultivate your wisdom, loving-kindness and compassion. So in whatever we do, try to be as mindful as possible with the view to cultivating healthy qualities. Whatever situation you may be in, try to respond with non-anger and non-delusion. This means to say we must respond with wisdom, loving-kindness and compassion.

In the present, you may try to have more material things or more money, in order to do more of the things you want to do so you will be happier. Unfortunate, life actually works is the reverse. You must first be who you really are, then do what you love to do, in order to have what you want. Your dream formula for success is this: Be intentional supportive and resourceful all the time, even during times when many have lost hope, dream big and take risks. Be bold and believe in yourselves. Believe that you can alter your life to achieve your heart's desire. Dreams are precious and essential and can change your family, community and the world. Your dreams can make you a better, more passionate person. No dream is too big or too small, it is only what is important to you and what are you willing to do about it. Doing nothing is not an option remembering that the world can always use another great leader who is willing to leave a legacy. Seek abundance and be abundant in spirit. Dream and dream big dreams. Don't give up on your big dreams! Your dreams may be fulfilled from out of nowhere and when that happens, enjoy the ride.

Thankfulness and gratitude are emotions. They are a duty, virtue, an excellence involving feeling, thought, and action. Gratitude is not just a thankful feeling or thought but a conscious action to express your joy. Gratitude is the sharing of your joy not out of responsibility or obligation but a genuine feeling of common, mutual positive emotion. To show your gratitude, you visit a friend and tell them they are appreciated. I have found that my appreciation visits provide an opportunity to enhance my life satisfaction emotionally and strengthen my relationships and bonds. You can begin to cultivate spiritual wealth by opening your hearts in gratitude. Your success will be multiplied with gratitude. Don't put it off, do it today. You deserve to be something, do something, and have something. Live all the days of your life in abundance.

Count Your Blessings Everyday and Be Thankful

You should be grateful and thankful for the blessings you receive. Every time you have a negative thought, countered that thought with one of gratitude. The more you contemplate your blessings, the more you feel the changes in your emotional attitude. The worst habit is ingratitude. If you feel gratitude, you will be amazed at the changes in yourself, your health, your relationships, your career and your life. You need to be aware of and thankful for the good things that happen; take time to express thanks.

Each day provides an opportunity to reflect on history, all the way back to 1621, the good old day as some of us may have read or been told. The Pilgrims had a hard and devastating first year in the New World, but the fall harvest was successful and plentiful. There was corn, fruits, vegetables, fish, and meat. The Pilgrim's had enough food to put away for the winter. They had beaten the odds and raised enough crops to keep them alive during the long winter. They were at peace with their Indian neighbors and a day was set aside so that all could share and celebrate. That celebration led to what we now call "A day to be thankful."

Since that initial sharing, Native American food has spread around the world. Nearly 70 percent of all crops grown today were originally cultivated by Native American peoples. One may sometimes wonder what tivated by Native American peoples. One may sometimes wonder what they ate in Europe before they met Native Americans. Spaghetti without tomatoes? Meat and potatoes without potatoes? And at the "first each day" the Native Americans provided most of the food and signed a treaty granting Pilgrims the right to the land at Plymouth, which may have been the real reason for the first each day.

On each day, we should take a moment to reflect history, the need to strengthen areas of our lives which help us to bond more with our families and friends and reflect on the priceless gifts we have been enjoying so that we can begin to cultivate an 'attitude of gratitude' in our lives. We all have reasons to be grateful, some more than others but it does not matter. For some, gratitude may be the inward feeling of kindness received. For others, thankfulness may be the natural impulse to express that feeling, which reminds us that we should learn from yesterday to live for today and hope for tomorrow, not just on this day but every day.

There is no purpose served in crying over spilled milk or what ever you favorite drink may be. We are now here today. When we find ourselves worrying about the past and becoming overly anxious, it would be more useful if we developed an attitude of gratitude and thankfulness. In recognition of a day to be thankful, it would be a good time to reflect and let your worries and anxieties go, let them drop naturally, effortlessly to the ground, continue on your way and as the Temptations sang "and don't look back." Life is a journey; as we continue on it, we must pick positive enriching thoughts to take the place of the negative thoughts that we let go along the way. If you don't replace a negative thought with a positive one, the negative thought like a bad habit, will return again. Thoughts, like dreams, are energized as soon as we project them into the universe. The longer you hold onto a thought or your dream, the more likely it will become a reality. Since that is the case, it is even more important for all of us to think positive thoughts because they will grow, just as a seed grows, if given enough sunlight.

Each and every day, we need to count our blessings. We need to set aside time each day to reflect on how fortunate we are, express our gratitude to supportive coworkers and family members. We need to shift our focus away from difficulties and nourish ourselves with positive thoughts, give them light and feed ourselves. I am often reminded that we should develop the habit of focusing on things that we are grateful for and cultivate an attitude of gratitude in our life. We should think about our blessings today and each day so that when the next time somebody asks us, how things are or if anything great happened to us today, we'll have plenty to say.

Carpe Diem and Seize Your Success

Remember that each of us has unique gifts, talents and capabilities. Our unique gifts make us stand out from the crowd. Many of us have heard the phrase, "Carpe Diem." But only a few experience it. Carpe diem is a Latin phrase literally meaning "pluck the day" but usually translated as "seize the day". It is often adopted and quoted as a personal motto. Carpe Diem is my motto, seize the day by planning to live by experiencing something new today. Seize the day by using our gifts, talents and capabilities to capture life's moments and live an extraordinary life. Carpe diem symbolizes the lessons my mother taught me.

Alfred D'Souza tells us, "For a long time it had seemed to me that life was about to begin - real life. But there was always some obstacle in the way. Something to be got through first, some unfinished business, time still to be served, a debt to be paid. Then life would begin. At last it dawned on me that these obstacles were my life."

None of us have been given unlimited time. If we keep waiting, we will never find time for anything. If we want time, we must make time. We all need to take that advice and begin to look at our options. Do we have to settle for hopefulness or can we develop our plan and work that extraordinary plan realizing that the only difference between ordinary and extraordinary is doing something extra. Be patient and be positive, knowing that our turn will come. Sometimes it is a matter of being at the "right place" or the "right time." We must live with a purpose and seize each moment, not because they will come only once and then disappear forever. That isn't always the case. But seizing each moment acknowledges all that we have been taught and by faith we believe. This moment on this planet is our gift and we should recognize each moment as a gift from God. And in honoring our parents and our ancestors, we should seize the day...and enjoy this day. No need to worry, none of us is perfect and there is no perfect day. But we can live perfectly in the moment. Acknowledge the positive side of this day from your perspective. Life was never promised to be easy and success will always uphill. So, hang in there and do what you can while you can in your life. Don't sweet the details.

More than anything else people seek happiness. Yet, few people have defined happiness and know what contributes to their happiness. I have found that happiness is not dependent on money or fame or power. It is also not the result of random chance. Happiness doesn't depend on outside events, but rather on how we interpret them. Happiness comes as a reward of being totally involved in living. Happiness is when we feel a sense of exhilaration, a deep sense of enjoyment that comes when our bodies and minds are stretched to their limits in a voluntary effort to accomplish something difficult and worthwhile. Obtaining happiness, personal growth and self-improvement, require the right type of environment devoid of anything that might induce anxiety or stress. We all need to get away from the struggle of time, step outside our routine and find that place where we can relax stress free, surrounded by people who inspire us on our carpe diem journey to happiness.

Principles

- You must be grateful for every opportunity remembering your mind can be changed and your actions must follow to achieve things that to date that have been elusive.
- Find your passion and your purpose will be a gratifying journey.

DREAM GREATNESS BE UNSTOPPABLE

CONCLUSION

"Black people have always been America's wilderness in search of a promised land."

— Cornel West, *Race Matters*

Having an exciting job, living in a big house in an exclusive neighborhood, having a significance partner will not bring real happiness. Real values are inner qualities that are not projected outward from material possession. When your work and relationships fulfill your passion, your work or relationships will reap its own rewards. Everyone deserves to be happy but you have to have a strategy based on your purpose and passion.

Constantly complaining with no actions won't help the situation. Ask yourself, "Is complaining about this helping me?" The answer invariably will be no. Then start asking yourself, "Is there productive action I could be taking to address this concern?" Repeatedly do this and taking initiative will lead to light at the end of the tunnel and your ultimate success. Don't get trapped by…"but what if it doesn't work out?" "What will everyone say about me then?" The fear of humiliation among our friends can suppress your dreams. Simply ask, "What is the likelihood that the thing I fear will come true?" And then, "If it does come true, will it really be as bad as I think?" Our minds tend to create "worst-case scenario." Even if no one is watching you, we fear failure.

Focus on the fantastic possibilities for creating the life of your dreams. You must understand what makes you feel dissatisfied and uncomfortable with where you with your job, relationship or situation. Then, you must align your thoughts and action to focus all your intentions on what makes you happy, something to run to, not just an excuse to run away. Don't get into the "Friday's happy hour" habit which masks your unhappiness and discontent with your job or relationship. Once you've figured out why you're unhappy, identify what really interests you, what is your passion. Develop a dream scenario in your head, ask, "Which of life would I like to have?" And "If I had to stay in this job or relationship, what would I want to change about it and what would I want to keep?" Dreaming greatness is the foundation to your action, but taking the first steps will still be difficult. You can make it easier by aligning your thinking and personality first. Then, you can rehearse the change you want to have in your life with your friends.

If you want to be successful, don't wait until you feel ready because no such time will come. Instead, commit to doing something that is aligned with your daily success goals. If your goal is to lose 10 pounds, you'll have to consistently deny your desires in order to achieve it. Successful people are not having fun all of the time. But they do feel empowered when they force themselves to do what's needed. Successful people are self-directed but you must also reward yourself for developing positive changes. You must embrace your need to change. Great athletes say a workout was good even when it hurts, "no pain no gain." Daily goals help to produce a masterpiece. Divide you plan into daily achievable goals. For example, imagine you are the sales representative who is selling something that costs two-thousand dollars. If you meet with twenty people before you make the sale, each of those meetings is still worth one-hundred dollars, the sale is just deferred. This is the only life you'll ever have, chose success not failure, look within to find your passion and choose to direct yourself towards the life you so deserve.

Excellence looks at the core of superiority and it begins within each of us. If we want to achieve our dream, we have to be about everyday excellence. Excellence is about having the right attitude and taking the right action. Attitude, action and appreciation form a cycle of excellence, since appreciation often stimulates, fosters, and encourages a better attitude. It all comes down to how we approach ourselves and how we interact with other people. Once we look for them, we find that the opportunities to practice and apply excellence in the workplace and in our personal lives occur minute-by-minute throughout the day. These moments comprise the heart of everyday excellence:

- The mechanisms that appear to prevent emerging women with potential from achieving excellence partially overlap with those that prevent women from rising from any step of the ladder.

- As leaders, we should set the standards for excellence. The excellence of any organization begins with individuals.

- We cannot talk about business or professional excellence without dealing with personal excellence.

- Having logical intelligence will give you a good start in succeeding in your job, but to be more effective you must also develop your emotional intelligence.

- Excellence is about raising the bar.

Conclusion

- We are born and here for two reasons: One, for spiritual growth, and two, to find our area of excellence.

- If we are to achieve personal excellence in our lives, we must be able to answer four questions…What do you love to do? What would you do for free? What comes easy to you but difficult to others? How do others view you?

- Be able to distinguish traits and characteristics of people who have achieved excellence as well as how you can become excellent.

- Leadership competency will help you to conduct a self-analysis of your personal quest for excellence and how it affects your professional quest for advancement.

- The composition of the work force continues to change, the need to understand and respond to people who are different than ourselves grows stronger.

- Research indicates that a major factor in employee satisfaction is the experience of being valued, trusted and respected, in an environment where people are secure in the knowledge that their efforts make a difference.

- Diversity is the condition of being diverse, variety. It is the commitment to meeting the needs of all. Differing from one another. Inclusion is the act of including, the state of being included. Inclusion fosters an environment that allows and encourages all individuals to contribute at their full capacity towards the achievement of goals and objectives. To include all, you need to understand that gender bias is the often unintentional and implicit differentiation between men and women situating one gender in a hierarchical position to the other.

- The results of stereotypical images of masculinity and femininity steering the assessment and selection process or the gendered structure of the organizational system, women is that they are not provided with opportunities to achieve their professional excellence.

You must be able to understand and be able to respond to gender issues such as: Are men and women essentially the same and is equality realized by equal treatment of men and women? Or are men and women essentially different from each other, whether by biological sex, or by historical traditions? Is equity realized by different treatment? Understand that both positions, "sameness" and "difference," can be interpreted as the extremes of a continuum; many scholars and policy-makers use a mixture of arguments depending on the context. Understand that research on gender and science is clearly inspired by both visions, sometimes focusing on sameness e.g. competencies, sometimes on differences e.g. gender differences in operational or behavioral issues. Here are some questions to ask yourself about your own emotional intelligence ask others to answer about you.

- Self-Awareness: Do you have an honest handle your own strengths and weaknesses, both in your field and in leadership? Are you able to read your own emotions? Are you clear about how you project them to others? Do you know if, how, and when your emotions enhance or hijack your thinking and decision-making?

- Self-Management: Do you have the ability to control your emotions, or do they often get the better of you? Can you adapt to change, roll with punches, keep calm in a storm, and keep a sense of optimism even when others are down? Do you know if, why, and how your words and actions inspire trust in others?

- Social Awareness: Do you have the ability to read the emotions of others? Do you react to the emotions of others in ways that make the situation better? Do you demonstrate genuine empathy — that is, a sense that you can see the world from some else's vantage point? Do your words and actions lead people to believe you are working in their best interest?

- Relationship Management: Do you provide feedback, guidance, and inspiration to others? Do you share a vision that people can see and want to be part of? Do you build bonds with people, webs of relationships, foster teamwork, cooperation, and collaboration?

There are a number of strategies for developing your emotional intelligence. The key is knowing yourself, finding out what your real desires and uniqueness are, and being able to live in a way that expresses your desires. Learn to be authentic, be honest in your behavior and speech, be true and spontaneous, express your inner feelings...understanding yourself and others and bring comfort to yourself. Increase your optimism when appropriate and beneficial. Develop an action plan to make specific changes. Become aware of your strengths and possible weaknesses and enhance your level of self-awareness of how you interact with others.

Read to improve your emotional intelligence (EQ). Draw from different people who are skilled in EQ concepts, approaches, and techniques, as well as their own. Develop the capacity to understand the other's point of view and possible distortions, flexibility for change, and work well with team collaboration. Become aware and in-touch with your feelings and thoughts and understand how they affect your behavior. Understand your feelings and use them to help you make self-fulfilling and empowering decisions and do not let your of anger and hostility emotions control your actions and led to avoidance, withdrawal, and sadness. Do not "blow-up" often or say things that are counterproductive because you are emotionally upset. Develop interpersonal skills and sustain harmonious, fulfilling relationships with others. Listening for the "lessons" of feelings: turn mistakes into energy. Identify your emotional intelligence competencies by asking skills by asking open-ended questions. Listening is the best way to get your point across. Increase positive feedback to yourself, to others. Learn to reframe negatives. Increase your appreciation of yourself and others. Just as I am the author of my book, you are the author and the finisher of your own life.

Principles

- Your past is a predictor of your future if you continue to doing the same things you've always done. You must change your attitude and behavior to facilitate greater physical, mental, emotional, and spiritual success in your life.

- You must take action and responsibility for programming your subconscious and conscious mind with dreams, positive thoughts and visualization. You must be aware of your intentions and ensure your actions are aligned to achieve all of your dreams.

AFTERTHOUGHTS

"Life is not a journey to the grave with the intention of arriving safely in a beautiful well-preserved body but rather a skid in broadside, thoroughly used up, totally worn out, and loudly proclaiming, 'Wow, what a ride!'"

—Anonymous

Few of us clearly know our purpose in life or reason for being "where we are" in life. But, if we observe how our lives unfold, and ask the right questions of ourselves, we will begin to understand — *why*. When we understand and intentionally align with our deepest reasons for being, we can tap into an internal energy source which becomes personal power and manifests itself as "passion." We each have the personal power to identify our motivation, values, virtues, qualities and talents, and each of us must align with a personal mission statement which provides meaning and fulfillment to our lives as we experience fun and abundance. We must creatively cultivate our passion and life's purpose with clearly defined intent.

As we form the habit of completing tasks and producing quality results, we gain additional insight into our life's purpose, the meaning of life, or our *raison d'etre*. Creativity is not a gift with which we are born. Most creative people *learn* how to be creative. Creativity comes with dreaming and seeing things differently and seeing different things, generating multiple options, breaking the rules, thinking and linking, being aware, knowing how you think, playing 'what ifs,' and trying something on for size. Creativity is enhanced taking steps towards enlightenment and learning how the mind works. We must make a conscious effort to choose how we spend precious time or waste time and lose it to mundane tasks. Ultimately, we will find ourselves acquiescing to someone else's expectations. By managing our time and controlling our thoughts, we create goals and plans that guarantee success. Along these lines, multi-tasking too often means that our own dreams, the dreams that bring meaning to our lives will never become reality. Now is the time to live life to the fullest. In order to find our purpose, we must take time to examine the story or "history" of our life. Our story has a big picture with many pieces that are interlocked with primary plots threaded through the years. By reflecting on one's life story, true self knowledge can be gained and that knowledge translates to "power." As we align our thoughts to our purpose, our lives will begin to flow in new and delightful ways.

The purpose of *Dream Greatness Be Unstoppable* was to stimulate interest on a topic that has been a joy to me for more than 10 years and suggest that people should look within, at their own desires and dreams. I hope that this book has helped you to learn about how to achieve success and bring you into perfect harmony with the laws of success. This book has identified life's themes your purpose driven life. Create a history map and/or write your life story on as few or as many pages as you choose. This process of self-discovery can be powerful in bringing meaning, ownership, and empowerment to your life. From this moment forward believe that you can achieve anything you could ever dream of. Whether you think you can or think you can't, it is up to you to choose how you think. No one else can do it for you. Don't allow anyone else to dissuade you from your intended goal. As my mother once said, "You can achieve anything you desire in life if you know what you want and how to get it." By doing this…I believe that good things you desire are on their way to your life. Cherish your dreams for they are the road map to your ultimate success. The key to your future resides inside you. When you cease to dream, you cease to live.

ABOUT THE AUTHOR

WILLIAM J. HUNTER'S PIONEERING WORK educates providers and patients on racial and ethnic health disparities, and examines the dynamics of cultural competency in eliminating health disparities. His theory and insistence that we must provide culturally responsive and equally, high quality care to all, is increasingly being recognized as an important health care mandate.

William J. Hunter is an author, public speaker, and business consultant His numerous articles, writings and columns as an editorial page writer and journalist reflect the range of his expertise. He is a doctoral candidate, Nova Southeastern University's Huizenga School of Business and Entrepreneurship and a Pi Alpha Alpha National Honor Society for Public Affairs and Administration inductee. He received his MPA from Baruch College (CUNY) and BA in Economics from Central Connecticut State University. He has served as a city manager in multiple jurisdictions from Alaska to Florida and assistant city manager in diverse jurisdictions from Arkansas to Connecticut. He was inducted into Central Connecticut's Athletic Hall of Fame for basketball. Previously, he served as host of WDRC FM 103/AM 1360 talk show and produced and hosted WVIT TV 30 NBC affiliate television public affairs show.

William Hunter has consulted for numerous national organizations on organizational development and effectiveness skills; knowledge management; training and facilitation skills; understanding of organizational culture; human capital diversity assessment; linking diversity, human capital, organizational goals; high impact diversity recruitment and retention strategies; cultural competency and customer satisfaction; and managing diversity proficiency. He has presented at hundreds of world-wide conferences and meetings and is an in-demand, keynote speaker. He has served on the faculty as an adjunct professor of Asnunutuck Community College Department of Business. Currently, he serves on a variety of advisory boards such as the National Advisory Team of Young Leaders Collegiate Academy of Georgia, National Forum for Black Public Administrators' "The Forum Magazine," National Urban Fellow Alumni Association, and Conference of Minority Public Administrators.

Dream Greatness Be Unstoppable contains the combined wisdom of philosophers, sages, leaders, innovators, communicators, scholars, personal coaches and everyday people with insight from multidisciplinary perspectives. William J. Hunter has a unique ability to share the "key secret ingredient strategies" used by top achieving professional. He also uses success stories to drive extraordinary levels of performance, joy and control over one's life. William J. Hunter wants to help you make your meeting a big hit this year. Humor is his gift. Motivation is his art. Wisdom is his calling. This is the essence of keynote speaker and seminar facilitator, William J. Hunter who is inspiring audiences across the nation. "To inspire excellence," says Hunter, "it takes optimism, confidence, and connecting with the hearts and souls of your audience." William Hunter displays these traits with a unique, motivational speaking style and he is gaining a national reputation for creating memorable experiences with his audiences. He uses wit to engage, entertain, and challenge his audiences. Then he delivers wisdom. The result is motivated people, empowered to excellence by Hunter's humor, inspiration, and wisdom.